MW00881903

ROME

AND THE

VATICAN

Easy

Sightseeing

Easy Visiting to Save Time
for Casual Walkers
Seniors & Wheelchair Riders

Guida Libri per Turisti Anziani e Disabili

ROME
AND THE
VATICAN

Easy

Sightseeing

*Easy Visiting to Save Time
for Casual Walkers
Seniors & Wheelchair Riders*

Guida Libri per Turisti Anziani e Disabili

By Donald H. Bowling, M. Ed.

Co-Authored, Edited, Book Design & Photographs by
Lorinda Ruddiman

To get additional copies of
Rome and the Vatican Easy Sightseeing, Florence Easy Sightseeing, Venice Easy Sightseeing, A Woodpecker in his Leg*, Voice Power*, and After Your First Six Words, I Know You*
order through www.amazon.com

*Available in Kindle

The author at the Pantheon in the center of Rome. Sturdy wheelchair ramp provides stable passage over two large steps.

CONTENTS

THE ROME AND VATICAN EASY SIGHTSEEING TRAVEL GUIDEBOOK

This guidebook for seasoned travelers, seniors and wheelchair riders would not have occurred without the help that was received from the following friends, family and businesses:

Ms. Lorinda Ruddiman of Lorinda Graphics, for the book design, photographs, map design, writing and editing, Napa, California.

Peggy Cartwright of San Francisco who is a writer, poet and pre-editor. She inspired Don Bowling to consider the importance of using good English language.

Mr. Jack Joyce of ITMB Publishing Ltd., 12300 Bridgeport Road, Richmond BC, Canada, V6VIJ5

Rick Steve's personal advice on helping senior citizen's and wheelchair users get comfortably around in Italy.

The staff of Green Line Tours of Rome who provided invaluable information on bus tours to Assisi and Orvieto, Italy.

Dr. Philip R. O'Connor, Ph.D. author of, A Loyola Rome Student's Guide to World War II in Rome & Italy, 1318 W. George Street #3C Chicago, Il. 60657

Last but most importantly, "Grazie!" to the wonderful people of Rome, Italy.

To Readers,

When I first visited Rome, I thought of a shining marble city with numerals like X, V and I, and gladiators at the Colosseum. This modern city of 3.5 million people, with many American cousins, had lots of Roman numerals carved in stone, a few shiny marble exteriors and lots of noisy car combat in the streets. Oh, the gladiators were still at the Colosseum but they were outside offering their services for photo opportunities with the tourists.

Rome is a mix of building styles: classical early Roman Empire, Renaissance, Baroque, and modern architecture. As you traverse around the city, it is densely built with one style built next to the other, sometimes patched in with a classical column on the corner and new brick and windows flowing out of it. Structures decay and new construction is implanted to upgrade decaying structures. This is a geographical area of earthquake activity making long-standing buildings work for their presence. The most notable buildings of this city are its over 900 churches that were built over many centuries since the Emperor Constantine (306-337). The thrifty Romans are recycling experts. Pieces of pre-Christian period architecture are often later recycled into the churches. Bringing stone hundreds of miles from the mountains was difficult at best and some of the marble was brought from other continents for its various colors.

The Romans even recycled Mussolini's 1942 World's Fair into the district called EUR (Esposizione Universale Roma). As a disabled person I am happy that they did. This very accessible residential and business district of Rome has marble and limestone buildings, and contains a magnificent model of ancient Rome (showing it during circa 300 AD) in the Museo della Civiltà Romana. This museum also contains lots of plaster casts of early Roman artifacts and rooms full of information of working aspects of early Rome to give the visitor a glimpse into the way of life of the people.

Travelers flock to Rome for religious interests, business, and cultural reasons but they never seem to have enough time to see the many important places. These places are everywhere and often only a few minutes from a metro stop, or spaced closely together, sometimes within yards of each other. Our plan for this book is to help you find the places you want to go quickly and save you time.

An airline flight officer once told me he flew to Rome every weekday and could never find any famous sights in his 4-hour lay-overs. I figured out that he was having coffee at a café that was a 10-minute walk from Trevi Fountain. With this example, I know I want everyone to be able to see all they can with the limited time while visiting Rome.

See you soon,

Don

Donald Bowling's 40-year career was a special education teacher of adults and disabled children.

Freize at EUR

Visitors enjoy the lake at Villa Borghese

INTRODUCTION

Every year the city of Rome and the Vatican beckon thousands of visitors from all over the world. If they are visiting for the first time, they don't know all that is possible to experience from this city's rich history. Often travelers come from faraway places and have limited time and resources. The plan for this book is to help the traveler to pre-plan their visit. Letting the traveler decide the areas of greater interest and focus on a smaller area of sights. This is useful if there is limited time, mobility or energy. We don't want to discourage anyone from visiting any sights, but you may want to limit your physical involvement to make your visit a little safer and an interesting experience.

The reasons for coming to Rome might be specific sights or special interests in art, archeology, religion, food, or even the people. Romans are wonderful, hospitable people who pride themselves in their amazing city and enjoy showing it off. It has so much to offer that you could spend several months here and still find something new everyday.

I just love the feel of Rome. It has its cosmopolitan feel because it is the capitol of Italy. The activity of the politicians in the city gives the air some excitement. The expensive black sedans mix with the double-decker tour buses. The barriers go up around a few of the government buildings when the parliament goes into session and the protesters make themselves heard. The military police (Carabinieri) work in this city alongside the city's police. They wear black and drive black marked vehicles. In the autumn of 2011, the riots in Rome were uncharacteristic of this city but marked the difference of opinion of the people with the elected officials and a change was put into place in the parliament. It was a short protest and the city soon settled down to the business of straightening out the country's finances and services.

The economy has tightened Italy's money supply as it has everywhere. The city is still open for business and ready to show off its stunning beauty. It is well worth the money and effort to arrive in this city to mingle with the Italians and share travel stories with other visitors. Don't be afraid to sample foods from the markets and the restaurants. This sunny climate delivers fresh and ripe produce. Visit the museums, they are numerous, busy places and filled with paintings and sculpture unlike anywhere in the world. The churches are everywhere and free to enter. Over the centuries, the artists and craftsmen have filled the churches with the best of their efforts. Rome should be noted for its unusually high number of churches. You can stand just about anywhere in the central older part of Rome and see a church. Most churches are grand, with ornate detailing and sculpture.

Each church has specific things that might interest visitors. You might find some parts of a saint that reside in the church, a beautiful altar, mosaics on the ceiling, stained glass, statues and final resting places of popes and dignitaries. Not all churches are open to the tourists and the respect of the local people needs consideration. They are there for the people who live locally and worship there. It is not uncommon on a weekend to see several weddings, baptisms, or funerals in many of the churches. The Italians, largely being Catholic and traditionalists carry one foot in the past and look to the future.

Upon my arrival in Rome it was obvious this was going to be a tough book to write. I knew I didn't need to hard sell the sights but it was going to be difficult to convey the visit here as doable for people who had difficulty getting around. The older Romans like to retire to the nearby suburbs for good reason. This is a city that is financially strapped and the upgrading to modern standards is slow to move forward. The city has bits and pieces of architecture from centuries of building. It is built together, upgraded, and added on wherever possible. Early architecture doesn't always lend itself to modern conveniences or ease in mobility, it might even convince people to unduly challenge their abilities.

So look for the path of least resistance and energy saving. Use a taxi when in doubt of your energy. Look at the distances and if it is steep. This is a city of hills. Main streets go up a hill, museums are build on hills, on the side of hills and on the other side of hills. How do you get there from wherever you are? Study the maps, look at the descriptions and consider the time and energy. Maybe rent a Segway or a horse and carriage to explore at a slower and easier pace? Then go and enjoy every bit of what you want to see.

If you are feeling adventuresome and energetic, try the buses or the metro. Notice the number of the people using the transportation and decide whether it is a good idea to use it or is it best to go to a café and wait for a later time when things are less busy? Do you think you can walk more and stroll along the Tiber River or over a bridge and visit the beautiful Trastevere area? It's a little south of the Vatican and has some beauty about it with its many trees and plants. There is a botanical garden that is a lovely place to sit and contemplate. If you get too hot or tired, you should simply stop and sit at a café. The atmosphere is quieter as is the pace of life.

The older center of Rome has many sights is crowded, busy and can be loud with the usual sirens passing by. It can be confusing with the crowds of people racing through the narrow streets looking for the fountains, churches and galleries. Just remember the sights are usually 600 to 300 meters apart. The area is not that big and the streets crisscross the area of 4 to 5 story buildings built close enough together that the parking is mostly for scooters and the lanes can only handle a small vehicle or motorbike. The rest is for just pedestrians to transverse. You may often feel like you are in a maze in this part of the city. Don't be surprised if you pass near a famous sight but don't exactly know where it is. You might have turned left instead of right? Passed the street that led to the piazza? An ornate street sign on the corner building or a small modern sign with many of the popular sights listed and arrows directing you only punctuate the convenience of knowing your location.

The Vatican, a country all on its own, still relies heavily on the city of Rome to work with it so that things can run smoothly and the tourists and pilgrims can safely arrive to visit the home of the Pope and Catholic faith. This grand complex of buildings was built with some of the materials of early temples in Rome and the galleries are furnished with art and antiquties from near and far. Much of the art is acquired by the church or given to it. They did a lot of work to beautifully display the art in the buildings. The male statues at the Vatican are all emasculated by a campaign that lasted 450 years of knocking off the stone penises and then placing and iron fig leaf over the area. Later the iron was replaced with a plaster fig leaf. The Popes felt these naked statues were a threat to the faithful.

At the end of a successful visit to Rome and the Vatican, you can feel sadness to leave such an amazing and beautiful historical place. Hopefully, you will feel satisfaction that you visited most of what you planned and that you learned quite a lot about Rome. You may never learn all there is to offer but you got to visit with the local people, tried their food, found out they are not so different and possibly very much like you.

Lorinda Ruddiman

The gladiator photos concession in front of theColosseum. It was fun to get a photo with a nicely costumed Roman.

View across Rome from the Capitoline Museum

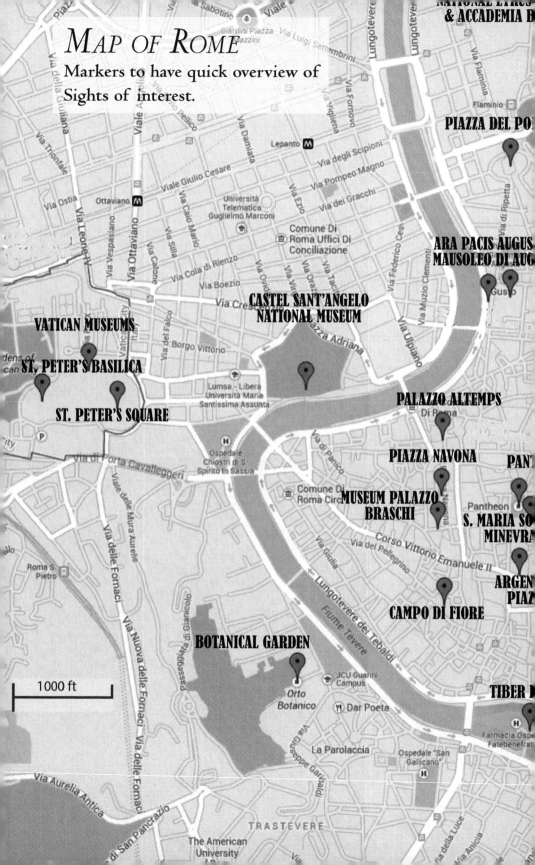

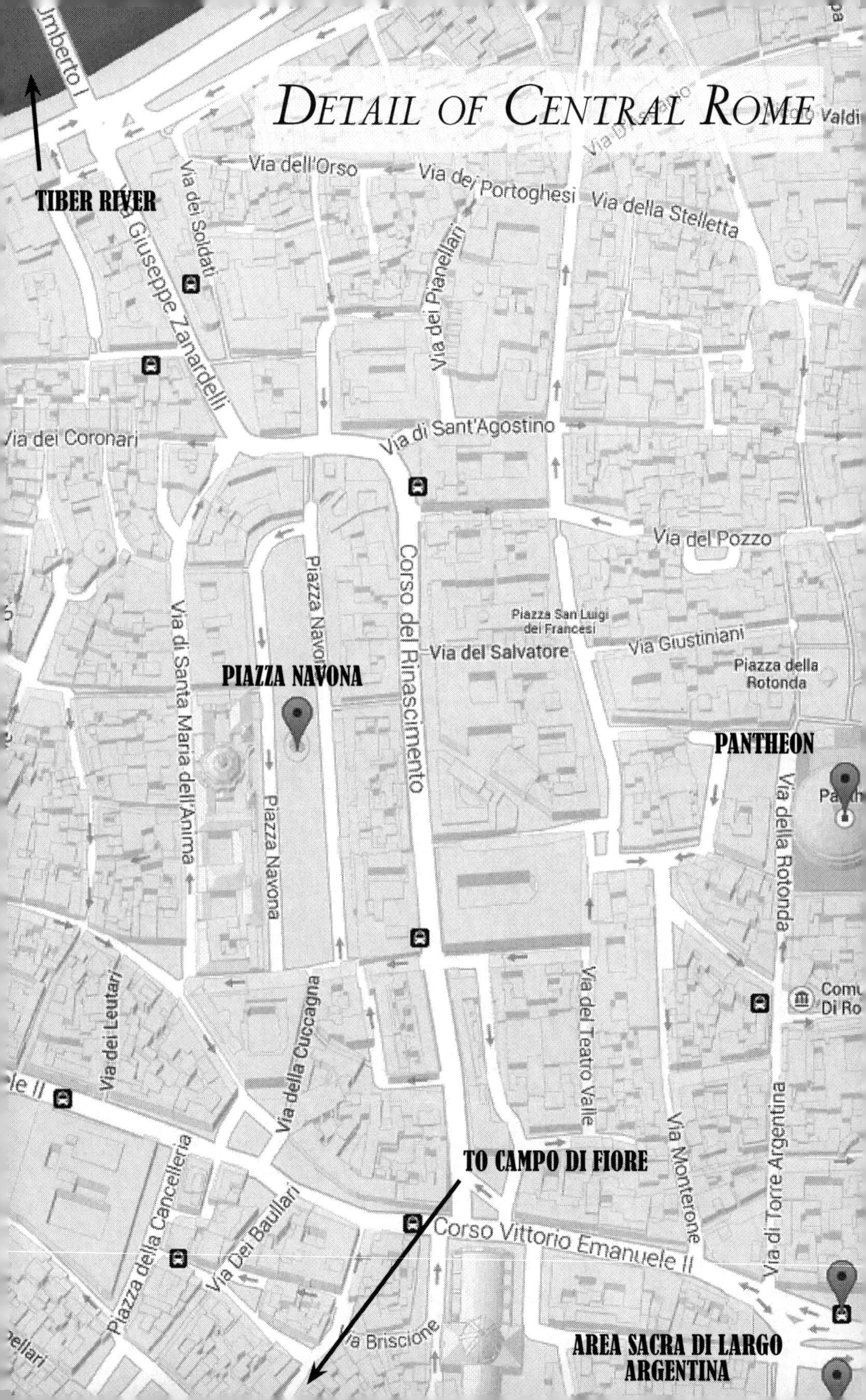

DETAIL OF CENTRAL ROME

Valdi

TIBER RIVER

Via dell'Orso

Via dei Portoghesi

Via della Stelletta

Via dei Soldati

Via Giuseppe Zanardelli

Via dei Pianellari

Via di Sant'Agostino

Via dei Coronari

Via del Pozzo

Corso del Rinascimento

Piazza San Luigi dei Francesi

Via Giustiniani

PIAZZA NAVONA

Piazza Navona

Via del Salvatore

Piazza della Rotonda

Via di Santa Maria dell'Anima

PANTHEON

Panth

Via della Rotonda

Via dei Leutari

Via della Cuccagna

Via del Teatro Valle

Comu Di Ro

le II

Piazza della Cancelleria

Via Dei Baullari

TO CAMPO DI FIORE

Via Monterone

Via di Torre Argentina

Corso Vittorio Emanuele II

Via Brisciono

AREA SACRA DI LARGO ARGENTINA

Multiple Buses Stop

Largo Torre Argentian

Buses from this station:
30, 40, 46, 62, 64, 70, 81, 87, 130F
186, 190F, 492, 571, 628, 916
agenziamobilita.roma.it

Trevi is the fountain that with a coin tossed in; it will ensure a return to Rome.

USEFUL INFORMATION

Traveling with a laptop, iPad or smartphone will help you to plan your trip more efficiently and easily as you go. You can reserve lodgings, tours, and passes in a few days in advance. Computers are very useful for reserving train travel and some museum reservations.

Here is a Rome sponsored site of passes:

http://www.romapass.it/?l=en

Use this site for the city buses:

http://www.atac.roma.it

Mobile version for buses:

http://www.muovi.roma.it

Website for pass connections and other tools of travel:

http://www.rometoolkit.com/transport/rome_travel_pass.htm

Website for sightseeing pass with OMNIA (private company in cooperation with Rome's museums and transportation:

http://www.romeandvaticanpass.com

Private guided tours are fun, informative and a chance to meet other travelers from around the world. Here are a few resources in no particular order that you can check out and see if they offer something you might enjoy. (we do not recommend any particular tours nor are we responsible for the tours or information of these parties websites)

http://www.romaroundtours.com/tours/

http://www.viator.com/Rome/d511-ttd

http://www.romexplorer.com/tours.html

http://www.city-sightseeing.com/tours/italy/rome.htm#tour-landingposition

http://www.vaticanguidedtour.com

http://www.romaround.com

http://www.romeprivateexcursions.com

https://www.privaterometourguide.com

One of the good websites for wheelchair travel in Rome with practical advice www.slowtrav.com/italy/accessible/rome/wheelchair.htm

- Churches, galleries, museums and monuments are listed in this book with information on how to find, enjoy them and learn about safer walking inside and out.
- Information to locate sights is shown on maps for easy locating and minimal walking.
- Rome's taxis, buses, metro trains and light rails provide the best regulated transport for this size city. It is also true that they experience rush hours and the buses and trains can be extremely crowded so it is important to understand this when planning your sightseeing.
- Travel health insurance can be purchased from airlines before leaving home. Often simple health needs can be seen to by the many pharmacies. Some pharmacists can help you to find a medical professional.
- This book describes shortcuts and accessibility routes that are written in italics to help the disabled and elderly.

ROMAN TRAFFIC

WATCH OUT FOR DRIVERS!

Don't expect the "zebra stripe" crosswalks to stop the Roman drivers from the sanctity of safely crossing the street. A lot of Roman drivers are driving 2 and 4-wheeled motor vehicles with their own rules.

If you have a green light, hope that the people walking with you are Roman pedestrians and you would be smart to follow them closely as they take command of the crossing areas.

What about the timing of signals at a busy street crossing? I timed the signals near the San Giovanni Metro Station. The crossing signal stayed green 13 to 18 seconds after 5 minutes of red. When the signal changed from red to yellow, I don't know if it was for the cars or the pedestrians; caution yellow went to green after $2^{1}/_{2}$ minutes.

The black steel pipes in the shape of an upside down U are handrails and may be difficult to see in the dark. They offer stability on pedestrian islands while you are waiting for the light to change, and act as a barrier from traffic.

The crossing signal control buttons on the posts are at waist level. Yellow rubber pads are there for the visually handicapped to help them stay the course and show the direction of foot traffic.

Watch for overeager drivers who want to turn in front of you when you have the right-of-way. Most drivers drive best when the police are standing nearby. Still you need to stay on guard and pay attention to traffic.

Emergency vehicles; ambulances (white top, lower half yellow and middle orange stripe), sky blue Polizia (some are Lamborghinis), black Carabinieri cars (national military police of Italy) and red fire trucks are abundant in Rome with blaring sirens and blue lights on top. Drivers and dispatchers often can speak some English, or find someone who does, and are very helpful.

US EMBASSY IN ROME

italy.usembassy.gov
Via Vittorio Veneto 121
00187 Rome, Italy
Tel. (+39) 06-46741 (switchboard)
Fax (+39) 06-488.2672

Directions: Americans who are searching for our embassy are usually trying to solve a problem. My problem was a stolen bag containing a credit card and passport. Take a taxi, bus or the metro A line, exiting at the Barbarini Station which will get you nearby. It's a two-story building about two blocks from the metro station.

Accessibility: Wheelchair accessible, the receptionist is on the second floor.

If you lose your passport, this is the place to go and it's $168 for a new one. They have a camera booth at the Embassy to take your photo.

EMERGENCY MEDICAL CARE

The medical telephone numbers listed below can get you help very quickly. Medicare or most private American medical insurances are not accepted in Italy, however American Express has an excellent plan called *Access America*. It is available at the time you purchase your airline tickets.

It is a reimbursement insurance that repays you for your medical expenses in the foreign country. It will even pay for your emergency return expenses if you have to return early.

Additional information can be obtained by calling before your trip 1- 800- 256 -AMEX.

EMERGENCY TELEPHONE NUMBERS IN ROME:

Automobile Assistance	Soccorso Stradale ACL	116
Ambulance, Red Cross	autoambulance Croce Rossa	06.5510
Ambulance, Helicopter	Eliambulanze	118
Blood Emergencies	Sangue	06.4456375
Emergency Services	Public Servizio Pubbilico Emergenza	113
Health Emergencies	Emergenza Sanitaria	118
Police Emergencies (Military Police)	Carabinieri	112
Police	Polizia Stadale	06.4686

THE IMPORTANCE OF GOOD COMMUNICATION

I think it is always important to learn a few easy words when visiting a city. It is so much friendlier to smile and say, "Grazie" to the person behind the counter who just scooped your gelato treat. Let them help you pronounce the names of the gelato flavors, it's fun! On a date with a Roman you can further the cause for diplomacy when you can say, ***"Buono notte!"*** "Good night!" Seriously, it is a step in the right direction.

USEFUL ITALIAN WORDS AND PHRASES

Buon girno	good morning	bwon jor-no
Buona serra	good afternoon	bwo-na serra
Buona notte	good night	bwo-na hnot-tay
Arrivederci	good bye	ah-ree-vah-der-chi
Ciao	hello or goodbye	chow
Dov'e il bagno?	Where's the restroom?	Do-vay il ban-yo
Quanto costa?	How much does it cost?	Quan-toe cos-ta
Un biglietto per favore	one ticket please	oon bee-yehl-toe pear fa vor-ray
Come sta?	How are you?	ko may sta?
Come si chama?	What's your name?	Ko-mah see-kee-ah-ma
Grazie	thank you	gra-tsee-ah
Mi chiamo	my name is	mee kee a mo
Per favore	please	pear fa vor- ray
Prego	you're welcome	pra go
Scusa	excuse me	sku za
Va bene	okay	va be nay
Si, No	yes, no	see, no

Websites for a few more Italian phrases:

http://www.learnalanguage.com/learn-italian/italian-phrases/italian-survival.php

http://www.linguanaut.com/english_italian.htm

http://translate.google.com/?tl=it#en/it/

Remember a sincere smile always goes a long way. Try to use these simple words when dealing with clerks, waiters, etc. They will appreciate your efforts. Italians like tourists to try their language and do not get upset with mistakes. In addition, they like to try American English, the language of their many cousins in the United States.

MORE FORMS OF COMMUNICATION

TELEPHONES

Pre-paid telephone cards make calling from public telephones a lot easier than fishing around for the correct change. These cards are mostly sold in tobacco shops.

Insert the card in the pay phones that have display screens. The screen shows how much time is left on the card.

CELLULAR PHONES

If you have a mobile phone, your company can arrange for your phone to work in Rome. Contact the service provider before you leave the United States and have them utilize the Rome satellite. Cell phones become just as easy to use in Rome as they are at home, maybe a little more expensive. Pay as you go cell phones are available.

INTERNET/WI-FI

If you have taken your laptop or iPad, you only have to choose a hotel with Wi-Fi and go through the hotel's wireless. Rome has many internet points, cafes and shops. If you use email at home, it is just as easy to use it in Italy. These places range from the back of a little store to a modern air-conditioned store. The 5 to 8 Euro/hour fee is cheaper than a telephone call to the United States. Ask for an English keyboard. Attendants are most helpful and will show you how to find the elusive @ sign on their keyboard.

During the busy tourist season you may find the store crowded with students waiting for signs of money from home. Once you have paid your money for a computer...the time is yours. Don't fret; the attendants will take care of impatient people who may want you to move on. Remember, in Italy impatience and rudeness is not rewarded.

Motorscooters are a common mode of transportation for the Romans. This postcard of the movie Roman Holiday was a fun reminder.

THE SHORT COURSE IN USING PUBLIC TRANSPORTATION IN ROME

Italy has fast economical and efficient passenger rail systems and buses. The large train stations are arranged so that the locomotives all head into the platform area.

Special assistance is given to the disabled upon a 24-hour notification. Special small trucks with fork-lift-like capabilities lift the person in the wheelchair up to the level of the train or take them down to the platform upon arrival. Tel. At Termini 06.4881726.

Directions from Rome: the station is easily reached by taxi, some of the buses or by the two city's metro subway lines A and B. These two lines intersect under the main Termini station.

STAZIONE TERMINI

(THE MAIN RAIL STATION OF ROME)
http://www.romaonline.net/Extras/Trasporti/fermate_trasp/termini.html
(this site is Italian only not English)

This transportation center of the city of Rome is more than just railroads. It's also a starting place for a hotels, taxis, buses, metro (subways), sightseeing buses, connection trains to the airport, a shopping mall and walking distance to important tourist sights.

Many old guidebooks warn about the dangers of city train stations. Termini provides a correction to this. It is typical of Italian rail stations; modern, clean and full of very busy working people, tourists and students getting ready to travel. In fact they resemble our better airports.

Metro lines A and B have their combined station here at the Termini. The Leonardo Express train leaves every 30 minutes to Fiumicino/Leonardo Da Vinci Airport, 16 miles west,(€9.50). Several trains (some high speed) travel to many Italian cities and nearby towns to complete the unity of this transportation station.

The station is large, modern and clean with a smooth marble floor that extends to the train platforms. Rubber pads about 3 feet wide are glued to the marble when leading to all-important sections of the two-stories of the station. These slightly bumpy pathways also have an occasional Braille directory placed on stands for the visually disabled. There are plenty of signs designating bathrooms. These bathrooms have attendants who usually collect 75 cents in Euros per person. This is a common practice in Europe that results in most bathrooms being extremely clean. They have a good supply of soap, tissue, and towels. Attendants open handicapped accessible toilets upon request.

The ground floor of the station is below street level and becomes the entrance to the metro system. Escalators are available to take individuals up to the first floor for exits, ticket offices and train platforms. There are a number of *"you are here"* signs throughout the station.

There are also **red emergency calling posts** that are about four feet tall and have a large button to push for reporting fires or calling for help.

Facing the train platforms you find the train station exit to the left. Taxis and ramp curbs for wheelchairs allow for easy and safe entrance and exit. To the right, facing the train platforms you find the busy streets of Rome. The front of the station has a public parking lot, bus stops and a more peaceful presence.

THE RAILROAD TOURIST INFORMATION OFFICE

These offices can be found in the station. They have an especially helpful staff that is proficient in most languages. There are free hotel directories that give up-to-date room rates, telephone numbers and addresses. There are special booklets available on accessibility in Rome at these offices. You should look for, *Roma Accessible Guida Turista per Persone con Disabilitia*, this booklet describes the accessibility of some tourist sights, hotels and churches in English. I recommend that you have your reservations before you leave the United States.

MASS TRANSIT IN ROME

THE METRO SYSTEM SUBWAY

Called *Metropolitana* by Italians, The Rome metro is a good way to get around fast. It is very crowded at rush hours. Most stations are below the surface and require stairs, escalators and elevators to reach the train station. Only a few elevators are unlocked. Help the disabled in Rome by writing to the transportation system. The metro stations are located by the colored M's.

There are Rome street maps for sale that also show where the metro stations are located In general, the two systems appear like a distorted X, consisting of an A train system and a B train system that cross each other under the train station. The A train seems better maintained and the car floors match the platform of the stations better for ease of wheelchair use. In general, I do not recommend the metro for wheelchair travel. Some of the stations are wheelchair accessible but not all of them, and with the new construction, some of the elevators and hallways are difficult to find but the metro police and workers are everywhere and willing to help direct you. Buses are better suited for accessibility and offer a view of the city as you ride. Taxis are more expensive but best for ease of use and quick, direct travel.

I recommend that Americans of all ages try the transportation systems. Take your time and don't rush for arriving trains. Pickpockets have been known to take advantage of the confusion of the rush on and off boarding but this are no worse than most metropolitan areas. The stairs are long and arduous. The Rome metro subway is good as any subway in the United States. The disadvantages are during the rush hours when it is crowded.

PURCHASING TICKETS

http://www.rome.info/transportation/tickets/

It's easy using the ticket sellers at the metro stations and the tobacco shops. At a metro station, you simply hold up the number

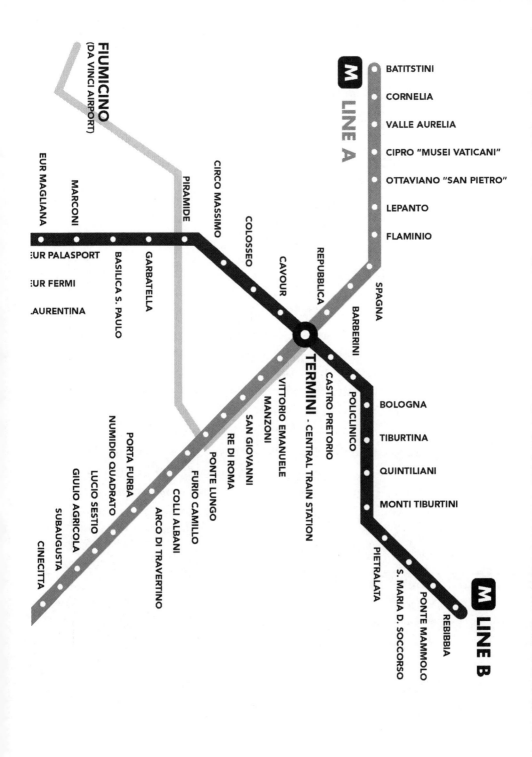

of fingers of tickets you want and they will dispense the number indicated. The stations also have machines and may take some skill to use them. Buy a few tickets at a time for future use or a pass.

When you approach the turnstile, insert your ticket in the slot and it will be time dated. You can then ride anywhere in the system a certain number of minutes but once you exit you cannot return on the train without purchasing another ticket. Buy the ticket for a 24-hour period. However if you lose your ticket or the time runs out, the honor police will give you another kind of ticket that costs $40. When you have seen your destination on the large map on the wall of the car, count the number of stops to that station as a backup if you cannot understand the Italian voice announcement.

ATAC AT THE TERMINI

The main bus station is located in front of Terminal, at Piazza Cinquecento. From here leave many city buses such as:

- 40 Express: Termini station - Saint Peter's (Vatican city)

- 64: Termini station - Saint Peter's (Vatican city)

- 910: Termini Station - Piazza della Repubblica - Via Pinciana (Villa Borghese)

- 110 is an open tour-bus with a jump on/jump off system to all major attractions in Rome. The visitor can stop at any of those sights. A ticket is €20. Departures are every 15 minutes. The Ryanair/Terravision bus to Ciampino Airport stops in Via Marsala, a street right behind the bus station.

ATAC METREBUS

THE BUS SYSTEM OF ROME

maps.google.com
www.atac.roma.it
www.muovi.roma.it - mobile version

Buses are well maintained. The wheelchair accessible buses are well marked and have a cage-like place to tie down your wheelchair. Buses are susceptible to traffic jams and the most packed bus I have ever traveled was a rush hour bus in Rome. Rush hours last a long time in Rome, especially in the afternoon. The price is very reasonable and you can purchase a ticket from a machine when you enter the bus. One way to use the system is to go online and list your nearest bus stop. www.atac.roma.it is useful for travelers who have their laptops, smart phones and ipad. It has an English translation which is a little difficult. Another way that is very good for the traveler is Google maps (English version). It gives the bus stops and directions by choosing the bus symbol and the locations.

TAXIS

Taxis offer a well-regulated system in Rome. Look for meters that print a receipt for you, avoid taxis that do not appear to be numbered or official looking.

Official cabs can be reasonably priced during the day and work-week. An additional surcharge is added on the weekends and evenings. A taxi fare within the city starts at €2.80 from 7 AM-10 PM, on Sundays at the same time it's €4, and at night, from €5.80. And if you're leaving from Termini, there's a €2 surcharge, plus there's a €1 charge per piece of luggage that has to go in the trunk.

You cannot hail a taxi from the sidewalk. You can order one from your hotel, bar or restaurant. Also, look for the posted taxi stops. If you are in a wheelchair, have the caller notify the taxi that you require wheelchair assistance. Your fare includes a service charge, so a tip should only be given for service by rounding up the fare. Carry a notebook and pencil to write down addresses for the taxi driver. Note; do not expect drivers to speak English.

WALKING OR MOVING AROUND IN WHEELCHAIRS IN ROME

Wheelchair riders should have pushers if possible as this is a busy city of hills and cobblestones. However, those near-walkers should try pushing their own chairs for better vision and training of the public to realize that wheelchairs can be a temporary condition. The new rough-terrain chairs should be a learning experience for everyone who sees the new arm propulsion method.

I try to use my wheelchair as an assisted walker device whenever I can. I make a special effort to cross the streets only at intersections with regular stop signs and some visible signs of the police. Traffic is as dangerous in Rome as it is in any large city but they do tend to make the pedestrians in crosswalks weave around the moving cars turning onto streets.

If you are able, walking is one of the best ways to taste the flavor, hear the language, and see the beauty of Rome. Window-shopping, sidewalk cafes, benches and walls help you rest and watch the busy life around you. Rome is an ancient city and more difficult than most to navigate because of the centuries old buildings and streets that lack wide, flat sidewalks and smooth surfaces. The older city center is dense and compact. There are small signs on the corners of walls to follow to sights. The transportation in this area is minimal and there are a few broad streets and mostly small walking streets (some small delivery trucks, motorbikes and small buses allowed), some of which have an incline and all of it is dense with visitors. The Trevi fountain is a very busy place packed with visitors, souvenir sellers and some police. It is located up a small incline from the Argentine transportation stops. Further up the hill is located the Spanish Steps. This area is equally busy and as many of the tourist areas in the city full of pushy sellers selling cheap goods and toys. So in an effort to make it easier on the traveler, it would be prudent to look at these sights starting at the top and heading down the hill. There is a metro station entrance right behind the Spanish Steps. So start there and work your way down. Give yourself time and let people walk around you while stopping often. Remember that these sights are often a few very short blocks, or less, from one another. It is worth seeing the beauty of some of these memorable sights and feeling the excitement of being a full participant of Rome's offerings.

OTHER FUN WAYS TO GET AROUND ROME

The Colosseum and Piazza Venezia, Piazza Navona and the Piazza Spagna (below) have horse-drawn carriage rides. These are a little expensive (about $25 - $100 depending on your negotiation skills) but give you a wonderful way to slow down and see people and architecture, while not worrying about the crowds or getting tired. If you get the chance to visit the Villa Borghese Garden, you can rent bicycles, surreys (pedal propelled 4-seater vehicles) or take a tram from in front of the zoo. The Garden is a large park that Romans enjoy with their children, family, dogs and friends. You can enjoy Segway tours here and in many places in Rome. www. italysegwaytours.com

Plaster of Paris
relief of soldier
at EUR museum

THE SHORT HISTORY OF ROME
WHY IS ROME LOCATED IN THIS
PART OF ITALY?

Professor James McGregor of the University of Georgia in his book, *Rome from the Ground Up*, provides a complete picture of the 3,600 years of the development of the city of Rome.

"Rome is not one city, but many, each with it's own history unfolding from a different center; now the trading port on the Tiber; now the Forum of antiquity; the Palatine of Imperial Rome to the Laterano Church of Christian ascendency; the Quirinal Palace beginning with the very shaping of the ground on which Rome first rose conjures all these cities, past and present, conducting the reader through time and space to the complex and shifting realities-architecture, historical, political, and social that constitutes Rome."

His rather poetic geological description of its formation:

"A southwest wind blew out of Africa. Behind it, at a slower pace, came Africa, itself. The breeze cooled as it crossed the ancestral Mediterranean and picked up moisture. Slipping over the Apennines, mountains which the African plate in its slow northeastern drift was heaving up. The clouds opened, heavy rain drenched the bare slopes, eroding and channeling, crafting a system of western-flowing streams. Not far from the base of these raw mountains, some 40 miles from the present coast of Italy, these new rivers the Tiber among them, after a steep flight down rock, flowed into a shallow bay of their natal sea."

"About two million years ago the steady thrust from Africa reached the sea floor beneath these shallow bays to open parallel cracks, volcanoes were born, Vesuvius and Etna.

At a spot now some 13 miles from the sea, the Tiber River came to a tongue of rock it could not scrape or melt away. At what would become Rome, the Tiber split, leaving a rocky island in midstream while it coursed through shallow rapids on either side."

THE EARLY TRIBES GATHER

"The west side of the Tiber River was originally occupied by a people called Etruscans when the Latins (Romans) began to settle in the present location of the city of Rome. Etruscans had been living for many years on the Arno River near present day Florence and the western half of the Italian Peninsula of the Apennine Mountains. Latin settlers began to move into Eastern Italy at the Tiber Island about 3,500 years ago. On its eastern margins, the Latin colony took root. They began to fill in the Albin Hills and Tiber Island when they met the Etruscans. Their common meeting point was the river ford below the island or shallow place in the river where early settlers could walk against the current as they carried on a trade in food and salt. Later, cattle were driven to slaughter and processing when the river was low.

The Etruscans, who have given their name to Tuscany, were more numerous than the Romans at that time. They were also more cosmopolitan and talented in trading goods and ideas with Greek colonists who had settled in Sicily and Southern Italy.

Initially the Etruscans dominated the Romans in their settlement. The leadership of the Etruscans was strong but the Romans learned quickly and eventually took over their settlement as they reached numerical superiority and a strong cultural identity. However, as proved true in later years the Romans adapted to the many Etruscan technical advances in stone construction. Fitted stones and creation of stone arches may have been inventions of the Etruscans.

Romans, however, continue to claim to have invented these and many inventions of the Greeks. Other technical advances of construction, design and written law could have been from the Etruscans and Greeks, but Roman historians and the Roman language development concealed how much the Romans copied. Later history shows that successful copy and development skills were to their advantage and to the development of Western Civilization."
Dr James MacGregor, *Rome, From the Ground Up.*

"At first the community was ruled under the established Etruscan Kings"

HOW ROME GOT IT'S NAME

In 75 BC The Roman Historian, Livy (In his Ab ur be incondita E1.4, 1-7) Wrote, (*translated from Latin*)**,** "Proca, king of the Latins, had two sons, Numitor and Amulius; at his death he passed on the crown to the older son, Numitor. Violence, however, overwhelmed the father's will and the morality of the era when Amulius deposed his brother Numitor and usurped his thrones. The usurper compounded his crimes by killing his brother's sons and condemning Rhea Silvia, Numitor's daughter, to a life of perpetual chastity as a vestal virgin".

"While he pretended to honor her in this way his real aim was to keep her from producing an heir. The founding of a city and empire whose greatness is second only to the divine must have been determined by fate, however, for Rhea Silvia gave birth to twins. She claimed the god Mars as the father of her sons, either because it was the truth or in an effort to excuse her crime. Still neither god or man could shield her or her children from the cruelty of the usurper."

"The priestess was bound and imprisoned; Amulius ordered her sons to be drowned in the Tiber. By the will of some god, the river had spread beyond its banks and flooded the "marshes so that the man assigned to kill the twins were unable to reach its main channel. And so as if by decree of the deposed Numitor, these men placed the twins in a wooden trough and set them adrift in a pool where a fig tree---anciently called the fig tree of Romulus—still stands. They were confident that the floodwaters would soon carry the boys to the swollen river, but they were mistaken."

"The Roman forum was an empty wilderness then. They say that when the pool where the boys were floating dried out and they rested on land again, a woodpecker brought them bits of food. A thirsty she-wolf coming from the nearby mountains saw the boys and ran toward them, the wolf nursed the boys and gently licked them with her tongue"

Author's Note: Notice the fluency of the Latin language of this time. The rest of the story is known to all, how the shepherd adopted the boys to live with him in the nearby Palatine Hill. Romulus kills his brother, establishes the city of Rome and becomes its first king.

SUCCESS OF THE ROMANS FOR THEIR CITY AND CIVILIZATION-

IT'S THE WATER, AND THE CEMENT.

"Rome began at a place in the Tiber River that was shallow enough to wade across at certain times of the year. This location had trading of: cattle, salt and agricultural goods, which led to constructing docks, bridges, and storage facilities. Eventually there was more trade with river and oceangoing ships.

For the blessings which nature supplies Rome, the people have added much with their own initiative. "If the Greeks are to be honored for their achievement as builders of cities that are renowned for their wealth, beauty, security and good harbors; the Romans must be counted superior in matters of their achievements. They designed the construction of roads, aqueducts, and sewers that wash out the filth of the city." Much of this built by Jewish slaves.

"They have so constructed the roads that run throughout their country by cutting through the hills and building up valleys, that their wagons can carry boatloads of goods."

"Water comes to the city in such quantities that veritable rivers flow through the city and the sewers; the infrastructure of their city" "Almost every house has cisterns, water pipes and abundant fountains."

"The sewers vaulted with close-fitting stones, had room in some places for wagons piled high with hay to pass through them." Strabo, Geography 5.3.8

More than 130 floods have been recorded during the history of Rome. The Muraglioni, the great walls built on the sides of the Tiber, have confined the River's waters a great deal. The first bridge built in 59 BC is in ruins from prior floods, but three others manage the flow of traffic. The building material for this later stone-age society was readily available from nature.

The Triumph of Sewers

Pliny, an ancient Roman scholar wrote in praise of the Cloaca Maximum (sewer), "the most praiseworthy work of all", and boasted that "it made Rome a city suspended in air that men could travel underneath in boats. Seven rivers flow through it united in a single channel. Their swift current like a mountain stream sweeps everything away." Quote, Pliny, Naturalist Histories 36.106. Pliny expressed that the Egyptian Pyramids bored him. He complained of their inefficiency and expensive nature but had admiration for the sewers of Rome. The sewer has lasted 700 years.

"A common sight on Rome's city street. Everyone uses them, it shows a trust in the quality of city water."

The Invention of Cement

The Romans had been using mortar to bind stone and brick together for centuries. It was only in the first century, however, that they discovered the way to make this mixture of sand and lime hard and durable enough to stand alone as a building materials. By adding a granular volcanic stone called pozzolano to their mortar along with stone or rubble, they invented a material that could be molded into virtually any shape and only grew stronger with age. As they mastered the new material, they found that they could make structures that would have been impossible using Hellenistic techniques. Late in the first century AD they began to elaborate on the plastic forms of their own architectural tradition in magnificent concrete buildings. The ceilings and dome interiors soon developed strength for a degree of beauty that had not existed until then.

FROM REPUBLIC TO EMPIRE, A SHORT TIMESCALE

Rome was a laboratory, in many ways, for experimenting with all forms of government. Rome had a powerful language and an effective level of education. A significant number of citizens possessed the necessary skills for self-government. However, the Republic demonstrated how wealth could corrupt democratic action. Men like Caesar lost patience with the games played by conservatives in the senate to block progress. He declared a lack of confidence in the practicality of groups picking the best decisions by declaring himself dictator. His assassination strengthened the drive to declare men Emperors. The resulting Imperial government from 27 BC to 475 AD demonstrates the weakness of such a government by looking at the Emperor's achievement and weaknesses as leaders;

- 100 BC-59 BC Julius Caesar rose to dictator and was assassinated.
- 27 BC-14 AD Augustus Emperor Rome's Golden Age of Literature.
- Jesus Christ born
- 62 AD Nero---starts fire to clean up city with Christians getting blamed."
- 81 AD Jerusalem destroyed by Titus. Vespasian starts building Colosseum.
- 98—118 AD General Trajan leads Roman Empire to its maximum size.
- 118—138 AD Roman Architecture best.
- 200 AD Roman Empire starts to decline in its effectiveness
- 272 AD Aurel begins last defense wall
- 284 AD   Diocletian & Maxmillian divide Empire between Rome and Byzantium.
- 313 AD   Constantine allows Christian religion.
- 331 AD Constantine makes Byzantium the capital of Roman Empire.
- 395 AD   Rome divides between East and West#
- 410 AD   City of Rome sacked by Gauls
- 493 AD   Goths establish their reign in Italy

THE WALLS OF DEFENSE THAT REMAIN IN ROME

SERVIAN WALL

Near the Termini Railway Station, a substantial section of Rome's red brick defense wall can be seen. It stands alone in a green island of trees and grass. The Servian wall, built of rough tufa blocks was about twelve feet thick originally and stood nearly thirty feet high. Its name reflects a Roman belief that it was built in the time of the Etruscan king, Servius Tullus. It actually dates from 392 BC. Some seven miles in length, it followed the contours of the land to form a defensive perimeter of the city and used till the time of Augustus.

AURELIAN WALL

Bus 85, passes through the middle of Rome, the Roman Forum, by San Giovanni Laterano and then passes through a large arch in the red brick Aurelian wall. The wall was built in 300 AD, almost 700 years after the Servian Wall. Built to counter the threat of invading barbarians. The city had been under siege for a couple hundred years by the maurading tribes of Germany and then the Huns led by Attilla. The wall follows the broken contour of the land, the brick-faced concrete wall forms an irregular circuit near- ly 18 miles long—the defensive perimeter of Rome at the height of its power. The emperors Aurelian and Probus committed vast resources to this project, and it was finished in only eight years

A step back in time to Ancient Rome. The view from the Colosseum towards the Palatine Hills on the left and the Roman Forum. The Arch of Constantine is on the far left and the Arch of Titus is in the middle down the central road.

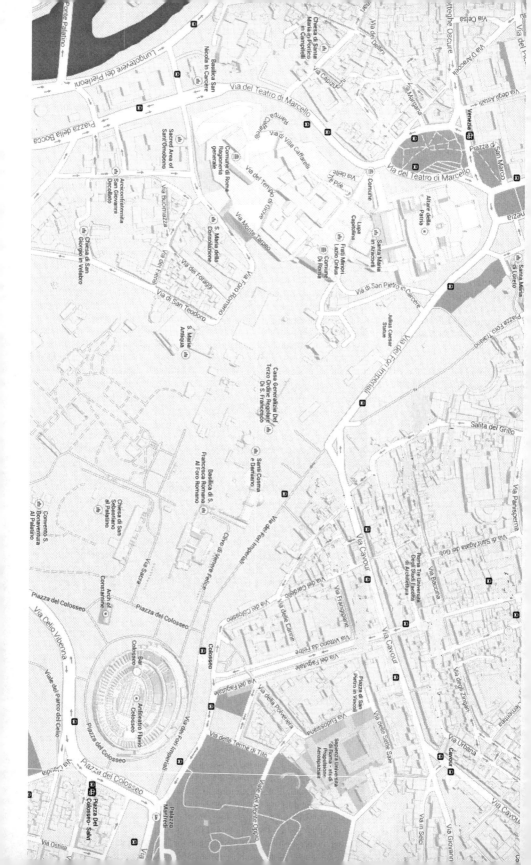

ANCIENT ROME
THE TOURS OF SEVERAL LIFETIMES

COLOSSEUM

THE ROMAN FORUM

TRAJAN'S MARKET AND COLUMN

http://www.tickitaly.com/galleries/archaeological-rome-pass.php

Use this website to purchase your pass ahead for many of Rome's archaeological sites. It is a week-long pass to multiple sites and museums in Rome. Use this to avoid standing in lines.

Ancient Rome began in the shade of a fig tree. It was originally nothing more than a meadow. The Forum symbolizes the growth of Rome over the first thousand years and its destructive appearance today demonstrates how the clash of early religion with Christianity created a furor to destroy the Forum's Greek-style temples to the many gods.

IL COLOSSEO - THE COLOSSEUM
Telephone 011 39 06.7004261
Admission: €7, English-speaking, small private tours for this and the nearby Palatine Hills available if you wait at the entrance (approx €20- €25).

Directions: metro line B, Colosseo station takes you close to the monument. A taxi to the entrance of the amphitheater is most convenient if you cannot ride the metro.

Leaving the front of the metro station, you can step down to an area of large flat square cobblestones. Going left about 1/8th of the Colosseum's circumference and can see the exit ahead. Another 1/8th of the way to the left and you can reach the entrance. A restroom is on your left by the Arch of Constantine.

Accessibility: There are two self-operating elevators that can take you to the second level of the stadium. These eliminate the need to climb 40 stone steps to the second level after you are in the building. There

are many other architectural barriers to tourists who have trouble with strenuous walking. The disabled need to take a taxi or a special tour bus to the Colosseum because the metro station is not accessible. Taxis or private cars with a disabled sticker can approach this non-automobile area from Via di San Gregorio. Turn onto Via Celia Vibenna and drive by the Arch of Constantine near the entrance. The entrances to the monument and the ticket office are on the south side of the structure. It also has a special entrance for the disabled.

Bus riders in Rome pass by this huge round edifice of arches and walls without a glance. This stadium was built for the people to help forget Nero and his hated Golden Palace and fire.

The Colosseum was completed and dedicated in 80 AD, a hundred years after the famous indoor Theater of Marcellus. It is more complex a structure that can hold up to 80,000 people with a series of concentric elliptical travertine supporting walls with a radiating series of concrete tunnels. Its continuous facade superimposed Greek architectural borders on three original arcaded bays. A fourth bay, pierced by square windows, was added by Titus after his father, Emperor Vespasian's, death. This top story supported tall wooden masts that anchored a moveable canvas sunshade that could be extended over the area; sailors manned them on perfor-

mance days.Romans provided the basic plan of today's stadiums with this design of sufficient exits for the crowds getting in and out of the structure efficiently. The arch was utilized in many ways to raise the structure up to an amazing height without the use of steel reinforcements. The Colosseum stands as a testimony to the building skills of Ancient Rome and its Jewish slaves.

Spectators and the emperor in the seats above the floor watched grisly public executions, simulated hunts for exotic animals or fights among sometimes-enormous troops of gladiators until the fifth century AD, staged hunts survived another hundred years.

The walls toward the south side suffered the most damage from earthquakes as they were warmer, heated by the sun. The rest of the damage came from invasions and the people of Rome who recycled the marble for building materials elsewhere in the city. The pope finally decided to declare it a Christian monument to protect it against further destruction. Don't let this stop you from visiting this structure and using your imagination to reconstruct its glory days.

FORO ROMANO – THE ROMAN FORUM

Largo Romolo e Remo 5

Tel. 01139.06.6990110

Directions: If you choose not to visit Palatine Hill, return to the Colosseum and start up the Via dei Fori Imperiali to **see** as many of the following sights as you have time.

Accessibility: The entrance off of Via dei Fori Imperiali is not very feasible for a wheelchair and not recommended. There is a steep descent at the entrance to the archaeological excavations. Wheelchair users can visit parts of the area if they have a strong escort or can use the chair as a walker at times.

Many parts of the historical area of the Roman Forum and Palatine Hills consist of steep paths, rough cobblestones and long jaunts. Much of this can be viewed from the smooth walkways above on the Via dei Fori Imperiali. This avenue links the Colosseum, Forum, Capitoline Hill and Vittorio Emmanuel II Monument. It is highly recommended if you have mobility problems to not go into this area and stay above on the Via dei Fori Imperiali. The heat and difficulty of the pathways needs strong consideration before attempting.

About 200 feet to the west of the Colosseum is the start of the Via Sacra at the Arch of Titus and the beginning of the Roman Forum. View the remaining marble columns and partial arches among the brick remains. There are rough cobblestone paths, rebuilt temples, forums and informational signs; enough remains are here to leave you in awe. The Museo della Civilta Romana at EUR (http://en.museociviltaromana.it) has a model of Rome at the time of Constantine, 306-337 AD, that was commissioned by Mussolini. The city of Rome has identified the location of the major edifices and provided trails, stairways and signs to give you a view of this ancient splendor.

There is a souvenir book that can help you see what this area

view towards the Palatine Hills

looked like at its peak. This "before and after" book with transparencies show its splendor. Ask for: Rome, Past and Present, Guide with Reconstructions. Published by Vision RS.R.L. Via Livorno, 20-00162 . Email: vision.sri@stm.it. about $10

As you walk by; look at the brick walls, free-standing columns, the twisted living remains of olive trees and realize that you are walking in the footsteps of the ancient citizens of Rome. Look at the Colosseum, "Can you hear the roar of the crowds?" This is your opportunity to be within "touching distance of the Roman Forum, Forum Nerva, Forum Augustus, Forum Caesar and an ancient shopping mall called the Trajan Market, you have just slipped back 2000 years.

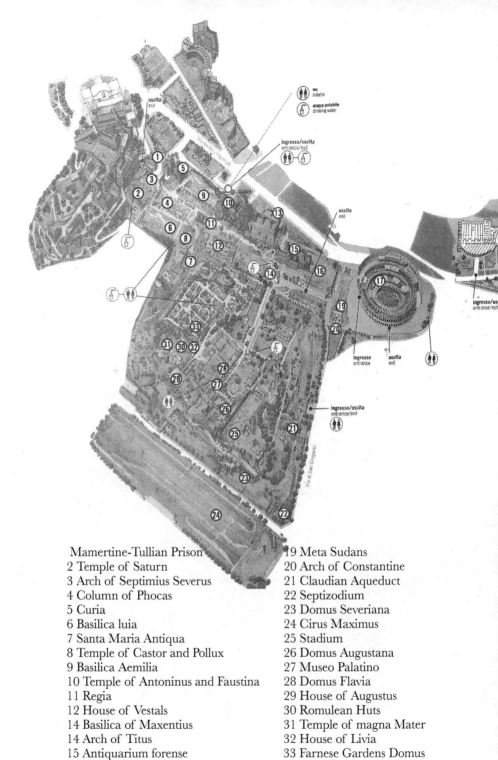

Mamertine-Tullian Prison
2 Temple of Saturn
3 Arch of Septimius Severus
4 Column of Phocas
5 Curia
6 Basilica Iuia
7 Santa Maria Antiqua
8 Temple of Castor and Pollux
9 Basilica Aemilia
10 Temple of Antoninus and Faustina
11 Regia
12 House of Vestals
14 Basilica of Maxentius
14 Arch of Titus
15 Antiquarium forense
16 Temple of Venus and Rome
17 Colosseum
18 Domus Aurea

19 Meta Sudans
20 Arch of Constantine
21 Claudian Aqueduct
22 Septizodium
23 Domus Severiana
24 Cirus Maximus
25 Stadium
26 Domus Augustana
27 Museo Palatino
28 Domus Flavia
29 House of Augustus
30 Romulean Huts
31 Temple of magna Mater
32 House of Livia
33 Farnese Gardens Domus
   Tiberiana

THE ARCH OF TITUS

This arch has illustrations of the sacking of Jerusalem by the Roman army. A special Jewish symbol can be seen in the relief carved in 81AD. This arch was supposedly built by captured Jewish prisoners and signifies the dispersal of the Hebrew tribes throughout the world. These Jewish slaves made sure they weren't forgotten by leaving the Menorah under the arch.

MONTE PALATINO - THE PALATINE HILLS

Via S. Bonaventura

Tel. 01139.06.6990110

Fax: 01139.06.6787689

Directions: Walk up Via Sacra. It is the road going up the hill to your left facing the Arch of Titus, Via S. Bonaventura.

Accessibility: This is a climbing challenge and some stairs, wheelchairs are not recommended. Electric golf carts are sometimes loaned. Reservations for carts require at least 7 days in advance. You may arrange this from home by using the telephone numbers or through your hotel when you first arrive. The service is available on Wednesdays and Saturdays from 10:00 A.M. to 12:00 P.M. and is free of charge. Elderly seniors can probably qualify for this service. At the entrance, the disabled visitor is required to sign a statement accepting all responsibility.

This hilly area contains the remains of Flavian's Palace, Domus Augustan, the Hippodrome, the House of Liva and the Farnese Gardens. The Palantine Hills are supposed to be the cradle of Rome. Throughout the Republican Era it was the living district of the nobles and the ruling class. During the time of the Emperors it was turned into a great monumental complex. Some of the noble occupants even had their own racetracks built to race chariots and horses. Today much of this is a few ruins and some foundations.

SIGHTS TO ENJOY WHILE A SHORT STROLL ALONG THE VIA DEI FORI IMPERIALI

THE ROMAN FORUM VIEWED FROM ABOVE

This is a great way to see everything on a wide flat sidewalk. Plenty of benches, room for walking assistance devices and wheelchair riders. There are plenty of vendors of all kinds here. You can buy food or cool drinks, souvenirs, and cheap toys from foreign vendors.

THE FORUM OF NEVI (FORO NEVI)

Directions: Continuing on the walk, a third of a mile from the Colosseum. Look down to the right from the railing along the road. Built in 98 AD it contains a remaining wall of the Temple of Minerva.

This sight is important to see because of its recent archeology project starting in 1995 that expose the many layers of Roman civilizations from 3rd century B.C. to 1930 A.D. This costly investment showed that this area of the city of Rome was occupied for thousands of years. Try to see if you can imagine what levels of civilizations lived in this area.

THE FORUM OF AUGUSTUS (FORO AUGUSTUS)

Directions: This location is a little past the Temple of Minerva and to the right. It was built to celebrate the defeat of the armies of Cassius and Brutus ("et tu Bruta?") in 42 BC. The Temple of Mars the Avenger is visible.

TRAJAN FORUM (FORO TRAINO)

Directions: Stroll a half-mile from the Colosseum and on the right side of the road.

This forum, built in 112 AD, was considered to be one of the architectural wonders of the world. Basilica Ulpia is nearby with a few columns visible.

This was the last Forum to be built. It was the most impressive of all the Forums. The complex had a main square, a basilica, two libraries and the Trajan Market described later. The Trajan's column, which presently stands 125 feet high, is widely described as one of the greatest pieces of art in Rome. The figures carved in relief around its circumference tell the tale of Trajan War Campaigns in present-day Romania. A replica of its many scenes of warfare can be seen up close at the Museum of Roman Civilization at EUR. Take the metro from the Colosseum

THE TRAJAN MARKET

Many centuries ago the market contained about 150 small shops in a two to six-story building. It was the equivalent of a first century Roman shopping mall. The conservative architecture of Trajan's Forum had no place in the commercial buildings behind it. Instead, the creators of Trajan's Market were free to work in the materials and the style of the Roman architectural revolution. This wonderful and imaginative complex responds to structural and social problems created by the Forum of Trajan. It replaces commercial space that may have been eliminated and acts as a retaining wall to shore up the slopes of the Quirinal Hill that were excavated as the forum was built. The rooms at its base are arranged in a semicircle that responds to the design of the forum. Their innovative forms in an extraordinary state of preservation make the market unique. Moving through them is like being in the best-preserved sections of Pompeii or Herculaneum; the sight rises above and all around, visually and emotionally rather than just imaginatively impressive.

Museo dei Fori Imperiali (closed Mondays) is located inside the Trajan's Market and houses artifacts from ancient Rome's forums. The modern entrance to Trajan's Market is on Via Quattro Novembre, 94, or Piazza Madonna di Loreto. At the end of the hall, a large balcony offers a beautiful view as does the exterior walkways of the building, of the Roman Forum, Palatine Hills, the Trajan's Forum, and the Vittorio Monument.

Descending the stairs to the sloping street, the overhead archways appear to have been turned on its side. Doors, windows, walls and pediments bend with the flow of semicylindrical walkways. With the exception of a few interior rooms used for secure storage, all these structures in their various shapes and orientations are both lit and heated by the sun.

Views from the Trajan Market
Top photo looks toward the Roman Forum.
Bottom photo looks towards the Vittorio Emanuele II monument.

THE CAPITOLINE HILL
THE MONUMENTO NAZIONALE A VITTORIO EMANUELE II - VITTORIO EMANUELE II MONUMENT
ALTARE DELLA PATRIA OR "IL VITTORIANO"

Summer: 09:30 - 19.30 (Fri & Sat until 23.30) Winter: 09:30 - 18.30 (Fri, Sat & Sun 19.30) Admission: free and €7 for the Quadrigas Terrace - for more panoramic views

You have reached the Venezia Piazza and, to your left, the front of the Capitoline hill but you won't see the hill very easily because of the gigantic white marble monument that faces the city and hills of Rome; the Vittorio Emanuele II Monument. It is so big it is very visible for miles across the city.

The front of the monument is not accessible but is to be viewed in its entire splendor. Italy's "tomb of the WWI unknown soldier" is guarded here and has a huge equestrian sculpture of Victor Emmanuel II and two statues of the goddess Victoria riding on a chariot. The monument, was designed by Giuseppe Sacconi at the end of the 19th century and completed in 1935 to honor the first king of a unified Italy.

The monument contains a museum of Italian Reunification; and a café, the entrance is on the right side as go around and behind the façade. It is worthwhile because you can get views of Rome from the nearly the top of the structure for free, and for a fee you can take an elevator to the very top to the Terrace of the Quadrigas' where you can enjoy more stunning panoramic views.

It has been a controversial building for several reasons: destroying a large area of the Capitoline Hill, too white, and too large, which all is true. However, it is still a considerable Roman landmark of splendor and receives many visitors. Locals compare its looks to a wedding cake or a typewriter.

MUSEI CAPITOLINI - CAPITOLINE MUSEUM

http://en.museicapitolini.org
Piazza del Campidoglio 1 - 00186 Roma
Admission: Adults: €12
Booking: +39 060608 (daily, from 9:00– 21:00)

Located on the top of the Capitoline hill and behind the V. Emmanuel Monument, it is one of the best museums of Rome. Be prepared to spend most, if not all day at this multi-level museum. There is art often from Rome or Roman collections; bronze statues were first donated by Pope Sixtus IV in 1471. The museum was inaugurated for the public in 1734. Many exhibits of early Roman clothing and housing are displayed for an education about the early Roman culture. The artworks of the many centuries are here and collected for their significance to Roman life. Some of Italy's greatest artists have some examples of their art here. The famous she-wolf with the babes Romulus and Remus bronze is here. The museum has wheelchair accessible toilets and a café on the top floor with its views of Rome's skyline.

Author's Note: A combination of; The Capitoline Museum, the EUR's Museum of the Roman Civilization (Italian "Museo della Civiltà Romana", and the National Museum of Rome will give the visitor a deeper understanding of Rome and the Roman's way of life and history. Each of these museums is recommended on their own special merits but as a group they are unparalleled. Each is located in different parts of the city so you would have to plan each on their own accord.

Above, steep ramp to Capitoline Museum on the top of the hill. There is a road on the back of the hill that taxis will take for people unable to climb the hill. Below, piazza in front of the Capitoline entrance. Left page, rooftop views of Rome from the Capitoline cafe's deck.

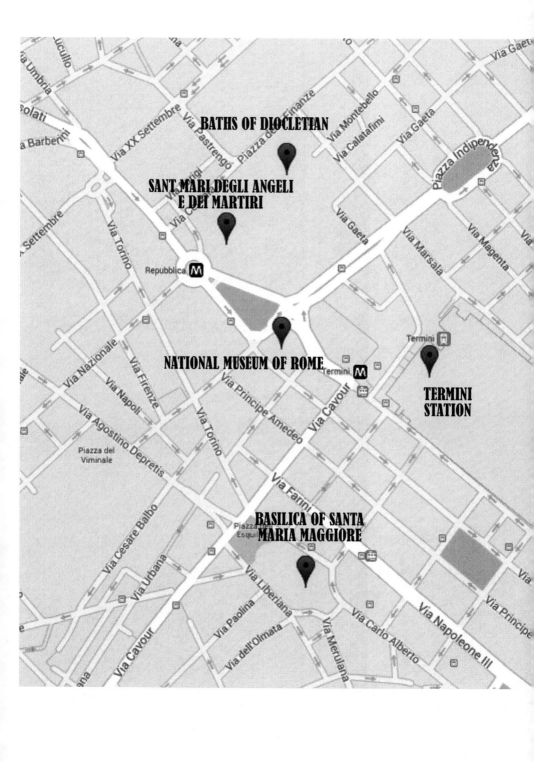

TERMINI NEIGHBORHOOD

NATIONAL MUSEUM OF ROME

Across the Piazza from the Termini Station is the Rome Museum that houses many famous art and historical pieces, many of which were unearthed in the greater Rome Metropolitan. Some of which were found while digging for the metro lines.

PALAZZO MASSIMO ALLE TERME MAIN BUILDING

http://archeoroma.beniculturali.it/en/museums/national-roman-museum-palazzo-massimo-alle-terme

Open every day, from 9.00 to 19.45, closed Mondays

Closed 1 Jan, 25 Dec.

The ticket office closes one hour before closing time.

Single ticket valid for 3 days at 4 sites (Palazzo Massimo, Palazzo Altemps, Crypta Balbi, Baths of Diocletian)

Full price: €7

Tel: 39.06.39967700

Accessibility: Wheelchair/handicapped entrance located to the right of the entrance at a door with a push button. This takes the wheelchair rider to a roomy elevator for access to all floors. The wide halls and open areas around the art works make for pleasant viewing. There are a few benches in some of the rooms for sitting, and viewing, or listening to the headphones explain the artworks. Restrooms for handicapped as well.

Spread over several locations, including the Baths of Diocletian, the Palazzo Altemps, the Palazzo Massimo, and the Crypta Balbi, the National Roman Museum at the Palazzo Massimo preserves coins, statues, sarcophagi, earthenware, frescoes, mosaics, jewelry, and other relics of Rome, from the imperial and Republican periods through medieval times. Many of the items on display were unearthed from the Roman and Imperial Fora as well as from outposts from the greater Roman Empire.

Some of the most interesting exhibits are the reconstructed decorated walls from early Roman houses.

The museum's present building was constructed in the neo-cinquecentesco style between 1883 and 1887 by the architect Camillo Pistrucci to house a Jesuit seminary. Recent renovations finished in 1998 upgraded the building to its modern splendor. There is an open center courtyard with large windows facing this charming light well. Visitors walk on smooth floors from room to room with open floor plans and entrances and exits. Exhibits are well displayed and lots of room around the artifacts and sculptures.

Above, front entrance of National Museum with several steps to navigate. Right, ground floor handicapped access to the right of the entrance steps.

BASILICA DI SANTA MARIA MAGGIORE

Piazza Santa Maria Maggiore.
06.483.195 or 06.483.058
Church: Free Admission
Museum: €3

Directions: metro trains A or B to Statione Termini are close to the cathedral. Walk four blocks southwest from the railway station on Via Cavour. Look for the Egyptian obelisk at the Piazza di Esquilino.

Accessibility: The interior is easily reached over the rough cobblestones in the front by a good ramp with handrails. Visitors need only to step over a ½ stone step to get to the level marble floor. The floor of this large building is flat except for the canopied entrance to a tomb that leads to many stone steps down. Santa Maria Maggiore has 6-sided chapels that require stepping up three steps to enter. They are worth seeing.

The flat wooden ceiling of this basilica has golden decorations that were installed by a Pope from Spain, Alexander VI. It is said that Ferdinand and Isabella contributed the gold, and more interesting, it was some of the first gold taken from the Incas of Peru. A visitor can see the twinkling of this valuable metal. Each visitor to this Cathedral finds remarkable art that has been added to its structure over the centuries. This author found Maria Major a favorite sight because of its nearness to Statione Termini and metro transportation. It is not crowded when one considers the importance of this church. It seems like one of the best-kept secrets of Rome

Tourists and pilgrims are encouraged to visit it as much as possible because of its location and sumptuous contents. Each time you visit you will find something else that makes this icon more of a special place. I personally spent a lot of return time looking at the 28 remarkable mosaics from the 5th century that is located from the altar to the front entrance of the Basilica. One mosaic specialist has said of this wonderful display, "they are examples of an art which had rediscovered a taste for vivid narrative, after accepting the rigidity of the late Empire." These panels start on the left side of the Chancel illustrating biblical events from Genesis, the stories of Rachel, Jacob, Pharaoh's daughter and Moses, the besieging of Jericho and the sun and moon standing still upon Gideon. Even if your appreciation of art is limited to the projects brought home by your children from school, you will find, as I did, excitement in the art of this magnificent church.

This most important cathedral was started in 358 AD, rebuilt several times and a bell tower added in the 14th century. It is one of the few ancient Basilicas that retain the core of its original structure. In other words you are seeing an interior that still contains design and structure that were present in all basilicas of the 1300s. Look at the wooden panels of the ceiling, most of the churches in Italy with wooden ceilings burned over this period. Consider the care that had to be taken to preserve these gold covered panels of wood.

A major ceremony involving the Pope occurs each August 15 on the Feast of the Assumption. A remarkable painted icon of the Virgin Mary in the Pauline chapel was used it is said, to stop a plague. Its painter was said to be St. Luke the Evangelist. A radio-carbon dating adds credence to this fact by indicating that it is at least 2,000 years old.

Gianlorenzo Bernini, sculptor, painter and architect who influenced the Italian Baroque, is buried here in an obscure and humble tomb under the altar, only a small brass plaque marks it.

In general, people are allowed to just walk here and there in the Basilica. I did not get overly concerned about the lack of handrails and found my own way of leaning against the wall to make up for the lack of control when I was going up and down the stair entrances to the chapels.

The perspective of the church's length is genuine. That is to say that there is no obvious manipulation of the distance between the columns to give a different perspective of the length to the interior of the church by shrinking the distance between columns.

It wasn't until after the year 1200 church builders like Michelangelo discovered that perspective manipulation of interiors was employed to give the churches more grandeur. In general the floor of the building is completely flat without any blocks from the front door that is about a six-inch step.

The bathrooms are located on the right side of the building wing about halfway between the front and the back columns. The bathrooms are antiquated but adequate. Accessibility is good when you consider that each of the chapels have only 3 steps to go up and over to get into the chapel.

The Statione Termini has many worthwhile tourist and religious sights. The order of visitation is up to the traveler and may be ended at several places.

Ramp for disabled use. This is typical of the ramps of public buildings around Rome.

There is no true facade; the simple entrance is set within one of the coved apses of a main space of the thermae in the Baths of Diocletian.

BASILICA SANTA MARIA DEGLI ANGELI E DEI MARTIRI THE BASILICA OF ST. MARY OF THE ANGELS AND THE MARTYRS -

http://www.santamariadegliangeliroma.it
Via Cernaia 9 - 00185 Roma
Tel (0039) 06488 0812
Fax (0039) 06487 0749
free entrance

Accessibility: The door is at street level with flat surfaces.

This church is located on the Piazza Republicca 3 blocks northwest of the Termini. The Piazza has a beautiful large fountain that is in front of the church called the Fountain of the Naiads. The entrance of the church is part of the ancient Roman baths of Diocletian.

The Roman baths were largest of the public baths built over the course of 8 years from 298. So the soaring transept vaults are part of the original structure and lend to the church's splendor. This was were Michelangelo spent his last years to adapt a section of the remaining structure of the baths to enclose a church. The interior is really beautiful with a special sundial designed by Francesco Bianchini, a scientist. It is a meridian line and helps the clergy predict an exact Easter. There is an oculus in one of the domes and a series of Galileo's experiments around the space.

In 2006, Polish-born sculptor Igor Mitoraj created new bronze doors as well as a statue of John the Baptist for the basilica.

The modern bronze door of the church.

In the Piazza della Repubblica is The Fountain of the Naiads is in front of the church with curved buildings around it. Today, this piazza is formed by the early shape of one of the wings of the enormous Baths of Diocletian. Below, part of the meridian line in the church.

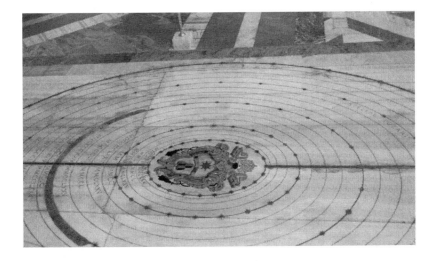

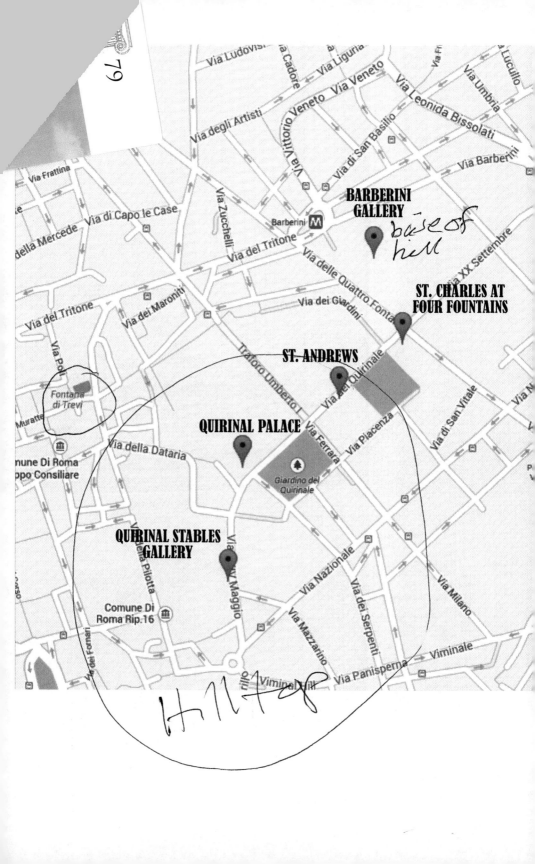

Barberini & Quirinal, Two Very Different Palaces

These palaces are near each other but the Quirinal is at the top of the hill and the Barberini is near the base. The Quirinal is the tallest hill of Rome's seven hills.

Accessibility: Steep hills at this point. This busy section of modern Rome requires the usual care in crossing the surface streets. The Piazza Barberini has a number of underground passageways to the Line A metro station that allows pedestrians to pass under the very busy automobile traffic. The station is at the base of the hill and very steep to climb up to the Barberini Palace. Wheelchair riders would be best served with a taxi to Barbarini Palace for a treat of many floors of paintings. Elevator access to all floors.

The Galleria National di Arte Antica can be found by going to the northwest up via delle IV Fontaine from the Piazza. Barberini Neighborhood is known for its elegant streets such as Via Venetia that winds through its rich environment.

The fountains of Trevi, Triton, and the Barberini family emblem of three bees, provide a remarkable décor most fashionable in Roman neighborhoods. The President's palace (Palazzo del Quirinale) is above and nearest the Fountain of Trevi.

GALLERIA DI NAZAIONALE DE ARTE ANTICA—BARBERINI GALLERY

http://www.galleriaborghese.it/barberini/en/einfo.htm

Via delle Quattro Fontane, 13

Tel. +39 06 32810

Tuesday to Sunday, from 8.30 AM - 7.00 PM, closed Monday, Dec. 25, Jan. 1

Ticket office closes one hour before gallery closes

Admission: €7

This was palace that now contains a museum. It belonged to the original Barberini family that produced one of the most significant Popes during the Baroque period of Rome's History.

Directions: Underground line A Barbarini metro station, walk about 150 paces to the left of the Cinema to Via Quatro Fontaine. It is suggested that you enter the large gate at the fountain in the parking lot as a short cut to the elevator. The surface is small gravel and easy to traverse.

Buses: 52, 53, 56, 58, 58/, 60, 61, 95, 116, 175, 492, 590

Accessibility: Some limitability with the location. The museum is facing a steep street. Wheelchair riders or limited walkers would do best to be dropped off on the flat driveway at the front of the building in a taxi. It begins with an exterior elevator that is two steps up. This elevator allows you to avoid an indoor flight of 30 large stone steps. There is a large bathroom area that is not accessible to wheelchairs.

This is an excellent gallery, well worth the visit. It is filled with paintings in 20 large rooms. Each room has a flat floor and chairs for resting and about a 1" stone lip to step over as you go from room to room. The Palace's salon has a remarkable ceiling painted in 1638 by Pietro da Cortona, a Baroque fresco of the "Allegory of Divine Providence and Barberini Power".

The two floors of paintings range from the 13th to the 16th centuries from all over the world. Most notable: Raphael's, *La Fornarina*; Tintoretto's, *Christ and the Adulteress*; Caravaggio's, *Narcis-*

sus and *Judith Cutting off the Head of Holofernes.*

The famous 3 bees shield below for the Barbarini papal symbol. Left photo, one of several gate posts at the entrance to the Barbarini Museum.

QUIRINAL HILL
PALAZZO DEL QUIRINALE - QUIRINAL PALACE

HOME OF THE PRESIDENT OF ITALY

Directions: Two blocks east of Piazza Barberini down Via della IV Fountaine.

Visiting Hours: 8:30 A.M. to 2:30 P.M. 2nd and 4th Sunday of each month

The Palace is open for interior tours only on Sundays. Photo I.D. is required.

The tour includes a succession of rooms, all decorated by Guido Reni.

Admission: €5

Reservations: None Required

Accessibility: The grounds and interior of the Palace are accessible to wheelchairs.

Individual visits rather than group tours are encouraged. The route of the visit on the first floor is completely accessible. At Scala del Mascarino (stairway) the attendants direct disabled visitors to an internal corridor making it possible to continue the visit without having to negotiate differences in levels.

A lift is available to take disabled visitors up to the first floor. This is preceded by a ramp situated about halfway along the "Manica lunga." The personnel are responsible for regulating the flow of visitors as far as the lift. At the end of the visit it is necessary to exit to the same point. The usable restroom is situated in the immediate vicinity of the left on the first floor.

Together with the long journey to and from the lift, the fact that there is no stop and rest during the visit makes it accessible only with great difficulty for those with restricted capacity for walking.

This governmental complex includes churches, palaces, ancient statues, an Egyptian Obelisk, fountains, honor guards of the Italian Republic and a general look at ancient Roman elegance.

Pope Gregory XI built this current papal palace in 1583 to have a location far away from the humidity and stench of the Tiber

River. It is located on the tallest hill of Rome's seven hills. Bernini and Michelangelo participated in its design and construction details. It has housed thirty popes, four kings and eleven presidents of the Italian Republic. It currently is the home of Italy's President. This location was once associated with the ancient emperors and gods of Rome.

The leaders of the church and the later kings and presidents of Italy built their palace in this higher cool air as a summer home. It eventually lead to the Quirinale, a Pope's, a King's and today, Italy's President's home. Bernini and Borromini designed churches San Andrea and San Carlino, to grace this area.

The Piazza Quirinal was embellished by Popes in the 16th century, moving antique statues from Constantine's Baths and basins from the Roman Forum in the 18th century. The Egyptian Obelisk was moved here from the mausoleum of Augustus.

SCUDERIE DEL QUIRINALE OR SCUDERIE PAPALI— QUIRINAL STABLES GALLERY

Across from the Palazzo del Quirinale, the 18th-century horse stables
Via XXIV Maggio,16
www.scuderiequirinale.it
Tel: +06 39967500
Open Sunday to Thursday 10AM – 8PM, Friday and Saturday 10AM - 10:30 PM
Admission: €10

Originally built for the pope's horses, this building has been transformed into an art gallery that hosts exceptional changing exhibitions. The stables were built on the site of the 3rd-century Temple of Serapis. Some of the ruins can still be seen from the glass-enclosed stairs overlooking a private garden.

SAN ANDREA AL QUIRINALES— THE CHURCH OF ST. ANDREWS

Via del Quirinale

Directions: Next to the Palazzo del Quirinale

Tel. 06.4744801 or 06.4883261

Open 6 AM – 6 PM

Accessibility: The church only requires climbing 3 steps at their entrances.

This church was built and designed by Bernini. His design style is opposite the style of the other church at Quirinale, San Carlo by Borromini. Bernini used a semicircular atrium in the church commissioned by Pope Innocent X in 1658.

The interior is elliptical like most Baroque designs but oriented on the shorter axis and defined by the entrance and the beautiful choir stairs. Bernini skillfully used colored marble, gilding and stucco figures to create a rich and beautiful décor. The second chapel contains three paintings by Baciccia

Raggi sculpted the white marble of Andrew tied to the cross before his crucifiction. Bernini combined painting, sculpture and architecture to visually create the idea of the devine elevation of St Andrew in this theater.

CHIESA DI SAN CARLO ALLE QUATTRO FONTANE -- THE CHURCH OF SAINT CHARLES AT THE FOUR FOUNTAINS

Via del Quirinale, 23

Tel. 06.488.3261

www.sancarlinoborromini.it

10 AM - 6 PM Monday - Friday

Directions: Located at the intersection of Via Quirinale & Via Delle Quattro Fontane

Accessibility: The entrance requires three steps.

The famous architect, Carlo Borromini designed Saint Carlino of Four Fountains in 1641. The dome should be seen to see the genius of his design. It is oval shaped and its coffers decrease in size as one looks up to give it an illusion of increased height. The lighting of the interior of the dome through hidden windows gives it the appearance of floating in mid-air.

Triton Fountain at the Barbarini Piazza

FOUNTAINS, FOUNTAINS EVERYWHERE

Water is seen flowing everywhere in Rome. Visitors from America may be concerned about the apparent waste of precious water and wonder, "Who left all the fountains running in Rome?" However, these visitors may have forgotten about the large numbers of backyard swimming pools in their own country.

The early Roman development of aqueducts started the use of this natural resource in public fountains, baths and remarkable sewer systems until about 600 AD when the invading Goths and other foreigners destroyed the bridge-like aqueducts that brought water from wells, springs and mountain rivers 25 miles away.

During the Renaissance a rebuilding of the aqueducts and a myriad of fountains resumed the waterworks. Gian Lorenzo Bernini created the *Fountain of the Four Rivers* in Piazza Navona, and his father, Pietro Bernini created the *Fountain of the Old Boat (Fontana della Barcaccia)* at Piazza Spagna. All this adds to the romance of the sculpture by Nicolo Salvi in 1762 of the Fountain of Trevi. Be prepared to see the many Roman fountains and their love for running water

FONTANA DI TREVI - TREVI FOUNTAIN

If you plan for a short downhill walk that is 350 yards away; visit the sights at the Quirinale first and leave the Quirinale Piazza heading northwest on Via delle Dataria, (it is a steep downward incline, go slowly) then turn right on Via di San Vincenzo and you will hear the fountain long before you see it!

If you are headed from the Patheon: It is located about 670 yards up an gentle incline of walking streets from the Pantheon, follow the signs posted on the building corners or just follow the crowds.

Accessibility: Crowded walkways to this area it would be best to approach from above and go down to the fountain. Very crowded with visitors and street vendors around the fountain.

There is a long history of this site where the current fountain stands. It has been many centuries in the making. The aqueduct that feeds it was first developed by Marcus Agrippa around 19 BC and this site was the termination point of the aqueduct. Less imposing fountains have been developed on this site in 1570. Pope Urbanus VIII decided to change that fountain's orientation to today's placement so he could see it from the Papal Palace on the Quirinal. That project with Gian Bernini was designed but never completed. Pope Clemens XII found a new designer in 1730, Nicola Salvi. Salvi died in 1751, the project was continued by Giuseppe Pannini and the statues of Agrippa and the Virgin were carved by Pietro Bracci. This massive fountain complex was completed in 1762.

It has inspired many films, the most famous being the 1954 movie, *Three Coins in the Fountain.* Also, Audrey Hepburn and Gregory Peck rode around this fountain on a scooter in the 1953 movie, *Roman Holiday.* Once there, you may ask yourself why am I here in this crowded piazza? The answer should be romance. The fountain offers you a promise. "If you stand with your back to the fountain and throw a coin over your shoulder, you may get your wish to return to Rome someday. "It's hard to resist. I certainly could not."

But to feel the true magic of this beautiful fountain, you must return at night. The crowds are smaller and the light show in the fountain is beautiful. Sit on the steps, watch the water and lights; it's a favorite place for lovers to meet. Venders appear selling a single red rose to the couples enjoying the beauty of this fountain.

It is always crowded at Trevi Fountain

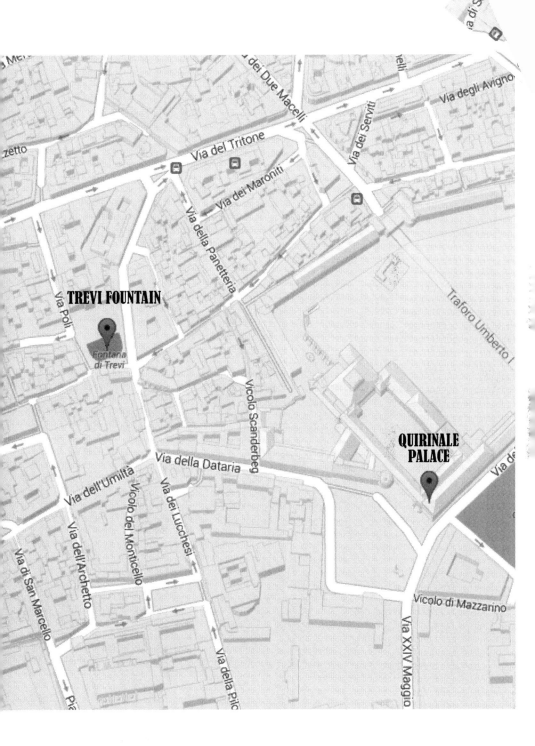

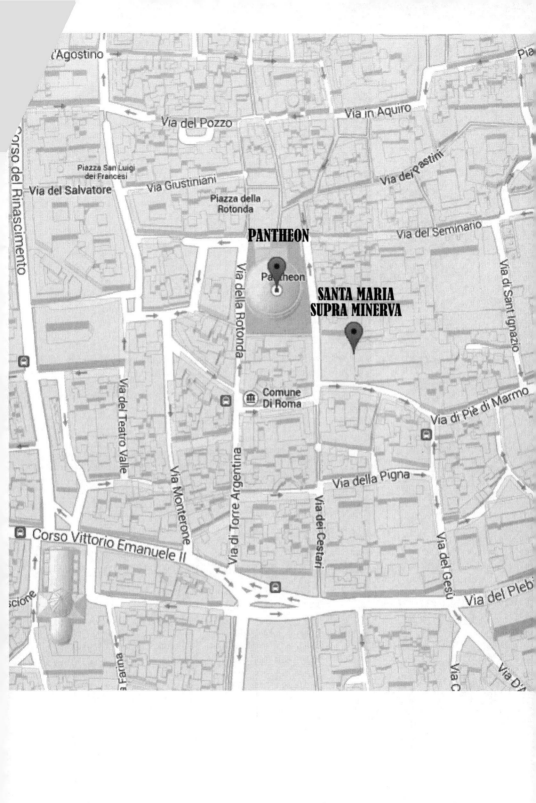

THE CITY CENTER
THE PANTHEON
Piazza dela Rotunda
Tel: 06.6830.0230
Visit seven days a week and the 7th Sunday after Easter to see an internal shower of red rose petals. Closed Christmas, New Year's and May 1.
Free Admission

Directions: The narrow streets of Ancient Rome where you find the Pantheon are far too narrow for buses. There is no metro station nearby. By bus, get off at the Piazza Argentina on Via Vittorio Emanuele II, a busy hub of bus stops and head 450 yards up either Via di Argentina or Via dei Cestari. Taxis can take you to the side of the Pantheon and drop you off.

Accessibility: The Piazza in front of the Rotunda is a large irregular cobblestone area providing a very bumpy ride to wheelchair users. It is recommended that wheelchair riders take a taxi to the Pantheon. There is a side ramp to bypass the 5 large stone steps at the entrance to the floor of the building. There have been many improvements and there are smooth asphalt areas on the sides and in front for better access.

The most important feature of the Pantheon is the fact that it is one of the few complete ancient Roman buildings remaining intact in all of Rome. Built in 126 AD and is presently in use for 1,890 years. It has a circular rotunda built with a domed ceiling and a round opening to the sky, called an oculus. It contains tombs of several Italian Kings, and the artist Raphael, also a church altar and sculpture and paintings. This extraordinary building competes with St. Peter's and the Colosseum for the most popular tourist sight.

Agrippa commissioned this building that has a perfectly spherical dome of 145 feet. This fact is stunning when you consider there were no computers; slide rules, bulldozers, cement trucks or anything we would use today to attempt a building of this type.

Night Life

The neighborhood and area surrounding the Pantheon is the location of a number of night- clubs and other entertainment places. This draws a large number of people, young and old to the area at night for typical Italian socializing. Hotel reservations near the Pantheon might guarantee an active nightlife if you have the energy.

Hadrian made further additions to this temple to all of the gods, from 118 to 125 AD. History hints of its magnificence when records show that its bronze portico, (entrance roof), was so large that in 1625, when it was removed, it was melted down into 80 cannons for the Castle San Angelo. In addition, its leftover bronze was used to make the four huge, twisted pillar supports for the gigantic canopy over the Tomb of St. Peter at the Vatican. Church leaders transformed the Pantheon into the Church of Santa Maria of the Martyrs in 608 A.D.

The age of the building is most apparent when you examine its rear exterior. However, the marble façade on the front with columns and pediment and the interior reflect an awe-inspiring church with altars and a number of religious art objects.

The 10-foot oculus, hole, in the center of the dome helps light the interior of the structure. It also helps the poured concrete structure withstand the stress of the weight of this huge hemisphere with no support from independent columns.

bust of Rafael at his tomb

SANTA MARIA SUPRA MINERVA

Piazza della Minerva, 42

Tel. 01139. 06.6793926

Directions: Walk to left side of the Pantheon, head right on Via della Minerva continue 220 yards, the charming elephant statue and obelisk, created by Bernini, is on your left in front of the church.

Accessibility: The interior of the church is easy to navigate until you reach the area behind the altar. The entrance has stairs. Wheelchair riders beware.

Foundations of the Temple of Minerva, Goddess of Wisdom, were used to start this Gothic church in 1280. It was changed and redecorated in the 16th and 20th centuries and contains medieval and renaissance tombs. This is the only complete gothic church in Rome. Upon entering the first thing you may notice is the beautiful deep blue painted ceiling, with gilded stars and red ribbing. Delicate arches and glass rose stained windows are just a few of the gothic trademarks. The church is also visited for its famous tombs.

The artwork of Beato Angelico (Fra Giovanni of Fiesole), Filippino Lippi, Michelangelo, and Gian Lorenzo Bernini are displayed in this beautiful church.

SIGNIFICANT TOMBS

St. Catherine of Siena, a churchwoman, was largely responsible for bringing the Roman Catholic Church leadership back from France in 1370. She is buried under the main altar.

Two of the most powerful Popes of the Renaissance are buried behind the altar. Leo X (Giovanni, 1513 – 1521) and Clement VII (Guidio de Medici, 1523 – 1534) were humanitarians and patrons of great artists, great politicians and men of many other great achievements in the church.

PIAZZA NAVONA
AND SURROUNDING AREA

Accessibility: The main streets near this piazza are Corso del Rinascimento amd Corso Vittorio Emanuele II. 52 yards on Via dei Canestrari from Rinascimento takes you into the south side of the piazza near the Museo di Roma (Palazzo Braschi). The single lane road encircling the piazza is restricted to foot traffic, horse-drawn carriages and some emergency vehicles. It has a sidewalk on the eastern side that can provide passage for wheelchairs. Bathrooms are available in the two museums and cafés.

Piazza Navona was originally the ancient Roman Stadium of Domitian, designed in 86 A.D. for chariot races. Thirty thousand spectators would reportedly witness the races. After the fall of the Empire, this large oblong space was made into a lake because of its concave surface. During the Middle Ages, the water cooled the Roman neighborhood and provided the crowds a place for boat racing. Shops, palaces and a church were built around it and the lake was eventually filled in and, during the Baroque period, became a cobblestone piazza that it is today.

Navona is a pedestrian area filled with beautiful fountains, artist's displays, street performers and tourists. The centerpiece of this piazza is Bernini's famous Fontana dei Quattro Fiumi or Fountain of the Four Rivers, topped by the Obelisk of Domitian. It was added 77 years after the two fountains on each side. There are plenty of benches in this public square to rest, and cafes ring the edge to sit, eat and watch the spectacle.

The two fountains, sculpted by Giacomo della Porta in 1574-5, are located on both sides of the Four Rivers Fountain. At the southern end is the Fontana del Moro with a basin and four Tritons. in 1673, Bernini added a statue of an African wrestling with a dolphin, to the Moro. The northern end of Navona is the Fountain of Neptune. The statue of Neptune was added in 1878 by Antonio Della Bitta to make the fountain more symmetrical with the Moro fountain.

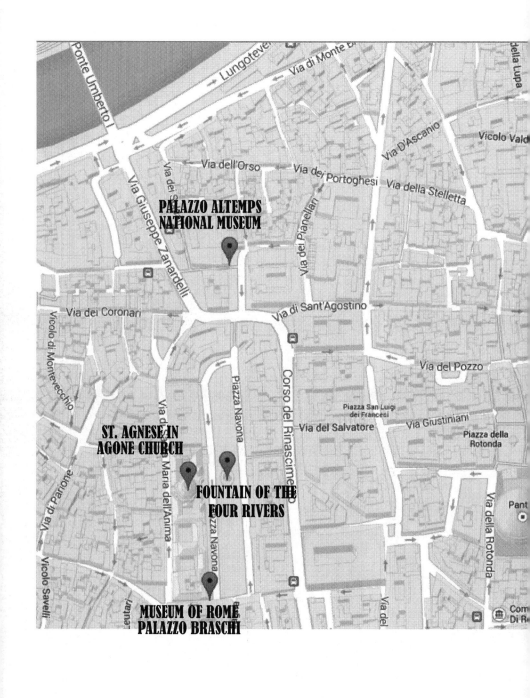

ST. AGNESE IN AGONE CHURCH

Directions: This beautiful Baroque church is on the Piazza Navona, behind the Fountain of the Four Rivers, on the west side.

Accessibility: The church requires climbing 10 large stone steps to enter. It is not always open to visit. This church is not accessible to wheelchairs.

The church has a striking interior with a smooth unobstructed floor. This church can provide visitors an interesting, cool place to rest during a hot summer day, when it is open.

St. Agnes was a virgin, martyred at only twelve years old in 304 AD. She is beloved to all Christians because of her courage and faith at the hands of her persecutors. A military officer wished

Agnes to marry his son, and on Agnes' refusal he condemned her to death. St. Agnes remained true to Christ, and pure of body and heart up to the time of her death. It is said that when St. Agnes was tied at the stake, the Romans were not able to light the pyre. One of the soldiers then cut off her head with his sword.

The Church of St. Agnes in Agony now stands on the spot where she was martyred at Navona. Her skull is exhibited through a round glass window at the altar of this church. The church is a popular pilgrimage for many Christians who revere St. Agnes and her youthful purity. St. Agnes Day is celebrated on January 21. Since her martyrdom several church buildings led up to the present church built in 1652.

PASQUINO, THE TALKING STATUE

Navona has related to the city of Rome as Hyde Park to London. Both are noted for free speech and protests against whatever was popular at the time. Just outside Navona and around the corner from the southwest end of the piazza is a small busy, traffic filled, square called Piazza di Pasquino. In it is the ancient 'speaking' statue of Pasquino, named for a nearby tailor who had a talent for lampooning speech. The ancient Greek statue buried in the mud of Navona was erected in 1501, Romans left lampoons or derogatory social commentary notes attached to the statue. Lacking a nose and arms, it was used as a kind of landmark to post anonymous messages critical of the leaders of the church government. Leaders began to consider throwing it into the river when very critical messages began to be attached during the night. A riotous mob developed as a result of one such notice about a new wine tax issued by the church government in the 17th century. As a result of a particular anonymous message critical of this tax, people were punished and the statue dumped in the river, then retrieved. Such was free speech in the Navona area of Baroque Rome.

MUSEO DI ROMA, PALAZZO BRASCHI
MUSEUM OF ROME

Piazza San Pantaleo, 10

http://en.museiincomuneroma.it/ne_fanno_parte/museo_di_roma

Tel. 01139.06.6875880

Admission: €6

Open: Tuesday-Sunday: 10 AM - 8 PM, Last admission 1 hour before closing time.

Closed: Mondays, December 24, 25 and 31, January 1, & May 1

Directions: Back of the building is located on the south end of Navona. Exit Navona on Via della Cuccagna walk to the end of the building, turn right and the museum entrance is there.

Accessibility: This structure has a ground floor entrance to the ticket booth. You can expect a smooth ride, with your wheelchair throughout the entire two floors. To get to the museum from the ticket office, there is a wheelchair lift to bypass the three large marble steps. The lift takes one to the base of another long series of marble steps. When your tickets are presented to the attendant, request the location of the self-operating elevator for seniors or disabled.

It would be wise to take the elevator to the top floor, #2, in order to spend the day going down back to the entrance. When you leave the elevator, on floor #2 remember where it opens. There are no signs to guide you back to this elevator door. The elevator can be found after touring 12 rooms. Both floors have handicapped accessible bathrooms

The art in this museum is outstanding and shows the artistic and social secular history of Rome from the Baroque to the Twentieth Century. It also contains early photographs of Rome. Some of the more significant art consist of:

- The Death of Achilles, painted by Gavin Hamilton, 1785
- Images of major church leaders and churches from the 17th to the 19th century

- Paintings of festivals and anniversaries representing the 18th century nobles
- Photographs showing the transition from Papal Rome to Rome the capital of the kingdom of Italy

This museum is very comfortable and worth the visit.

PALAZZO ALTEMPS NATIONAL MUSEUM

Piazza di Sant'Apollinare, 46
Tel. +39 06 3996 7700
Archeoroma.beniculturali.it
Open every day from 9 AM - 7:45 PM
Closed Mondays (except Easter Monday and during the "Culture Week"), Jan. 1, Dec. 25
The Ticket Office closes one hour before closing time.
Single ticket valid for 3 days at 4 sites (Palazzo Massimo, Palazzo Altemps, Baths of Diocletian, Crypta Balbi)
Full price: € 7

Directions: Walk to the north end of the Piazza Navona, continue on to Via Agonale, turn right onto Via di Sant'Agostino, turn left onto Piazza di Sant'Apollinare, turn left onto Via di Sant'Apollinare arrive at Palazzo Altemps. Total distance is 142 yards from Navona.

Accessibility: This 15th century palace has an accessible entrance with only one small stone step to cross. It has bathrooms that the handicapped can use with assistance. There is a service elevator to take seniors and wheelchair users to the second floor upon request. There are many benches for resting.

This two-story museum houses many ancient Greek and Roman Statues with the important Ludovisi, Mattei and Altemps Collections. This restored Renaissance Palace contains one of Rome's finest collections of marble. Most interesting are the descriptions of how these statues were repaired and protected during a time when the city was constantly under attacked.

The south Loggia upstairs shows a 20 AD bas-relief of several Gods and Goddesses at play on Mt. Olympus. Vulcan, Mars, Venus, Apollo Hercules, Bacchus Mercury and Luna

A rather strange looking Julius Caesar is shown In the Hall of Portraits compared to a "heroic" looking Marcus Aurelius, the philosopher.

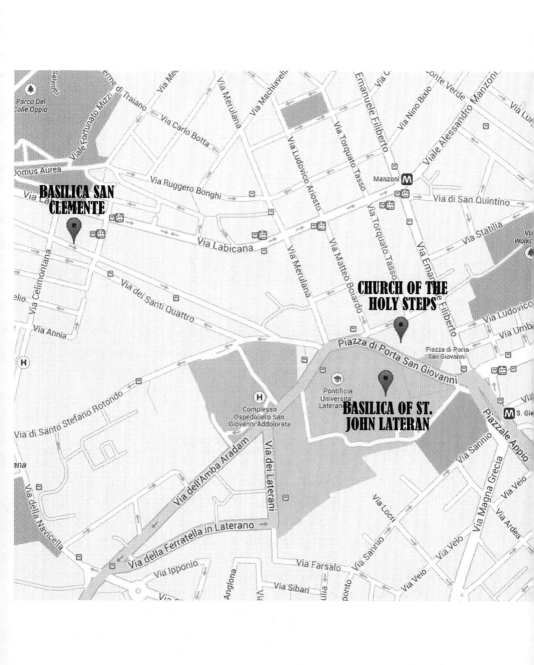

SAN GIOVANNI NEIGHBORHOOD
INTERESTING OLDER CHURCHES

BASILICA DI SAN GIOVANNI IN LATERANO--BASILICA OF ST. JOHN LATERAN

THE POPE'S CHURCH

Piazza di San Giovanni in Laterano

Open daily from 7:00 to 19:00, in winter until 18:00.

Free entrance.

Tel: +39 06 7720 7991

Entrance to the Church's Museum: €2

Directions: Take metro A to station San Giovanni. Turn left from the station's exit and go through the portal of the 3rd century wall of the City of Rome. Depending upon if you ride a wheelchair, you may want to take a taxi directly to the San Giovanni in Laterano Church.

Accessibility: The paving of the two large piazzas in front of the basilica are made from large flat square cobblestones for easy walking. Inside there are a few steps on the left side of the building that makes wheelchair movement difficult. The floor is mostly smooth and flat with occasional steps up to the Pope's altar and other side chapels. The entrance from the Piazza di Porta San Giovanni is sometimes inaccessible. However, an alternate entrance from the back at the Piazza San Giovanni has a well-placed ramp for wheelchairs with only one stone step to climb.

Emperor Constantine started building this religious center in about 320 AD. It has been rebuilt many times into its present magnificence. Earthquakes and the invasions by barbarians for centuries continually devastated the building. It was continually rebuilt, repaired, enlarged and became adorned with its present paintings, statuary and mosaics. The north facade of the exterior was designed in 1586 by Fontana who added Rome's tallest Egyptian Obelisk to the area. The chapels surrounding the Baptismal Font have mosaics from the sixth century.

The huge bronze doors are supposed to have been taken from the Ancient Baths of Caracalla. San Giovanni Laterano could have been the Vatican of today. It was seen as one of the most important religious centers in Rome until 1929, when agreement between the church and the Italian Government settled on the Vatican and St. Peter's Basilica being a special religious country. This Lateran Treaty ended the government's competition with church power in many parts of Italy and focused it on the present city/state of the Vatican.

San Giovanni Laterano is more important of the churches in Italy and Rome. There are many sacred relics here that add to its importance. There is several icons related to St. John the Evangelist: the Chalice from which he drank poison, the chain with which he was bound and the miraculous tunic he used to raise three people from the dead. Some of the other relics are the sackcloth of John the Baptist, the cloth Jesus used to dry the feet of his disciples and the red garment Jesus was given by the soldiers of Pontius Pilate. Remains of the heads of Peter and Paul were also sent as an indicator of the high significance of Laterano.

THE POPE'S PALACE

The palace next to the Basilica provided shelter for many during the German occupation of Rome in 1944 and 1945. There were hundreds of Italian Partisans, Jews, and escaped American and English Prisoners of War that were hidden by the church during this period. A visit to the San Giovanni area with its basilica, and Palace shows an area that could have been the location of the present day Vatican. Each Basilica in Rome and their relative isolation from St. Peters demonstrates the sacrifice made by the church in the 1929 agreement with the nation of Italy to assist in its drive to become a truly united nation.

The grand size and splendor of San Giovanni

SANTUARIO DELLA SCALE SANTA-- CHURCH OF THE HOLY STEPS

Piazza S. Giovanni Laterano 14
Tel: 01139.06.3202871
Admission: Free
Santa Sanctorum: €3,50

Directions: Look across the piazza in front of the Basilica. The rectangular Gothic building with 7 steps and 5 arches in front can be seen. The non-religious looking building with the remains of Nero's aqueduct on its left is very visible.

Accessibility: The church is not accessible to wheelchairs. Secular ambulatory visitors can climb a parallel flight of stairs to see this remarkable old church. Some pilgrims choose to climb the twenty-eight wood covered stone steps on their knees.

A very important 7th century sanctuary is found on the upper floor of this building. These flights of 28 stone steps were reputed to be the same steps that Jesus Christ climbed to be judged by Pontius Pilate. The mother of the first Christian Emperor of Rome (Helena) had them brought from the Villa of Pilate in Jerusalem in the 4th century to this location.

One very old piece of art says that this is the most holy Christian place in the world. The first private chapel of the Popes contains a very holy picture of Christ called the Redeemer or Acheiropoieta (miraculous image appeared and not painted by human hands). The sanctuary is accompanied by a number of chapels and a number of frescoes, mosaics and statues. The four evangelists, Matthew, Mark, Luke and John are shown as angels with the heads of a human, lion, bull and eagle. Pilgrims will probably want to spend a great amount of time in this very special place.

BASILICA DI SAN CLEMENTE-CHURCH OF THE SAN CLEMENTE

Piazza S. Clemente
Tel: +06.774.0021
Information for the excavations: Monday to Saturday, 9 -12:30 &
3 -6 PM Last entrance to the excavations at 12.10 & 5.40 PM. On
Sundays and State Holidays, 12-6 Last entrance to the excavations at 5:40 PM. Admission to the excavations – €5 Admission for
students under 26 years of age, with student's I.D., – €3,50

http://www.basilicasanclemente.com

Directions: One way to reach San Clemente is to walk northwest
along the Via di San Giovanni in Laterano after leaving S. Andrea
della Valle for about 15 minutes.

San Clemente can be reached by walking 10 minutes east on Via
Labicana from line B metro, Colosseo Station by the Colosseum.

This church is notable for its grand frescos and 12th century mosaics. The gold leaf tiles glitter while the stone mosaic of peacocks
in tantilizing blues is quite unusual. This 4th century basilica has
a mosiac in its dome that shows the cross as the Tree of Life. San
Clemente is the only gothic church in Rome and is kind of like a
Basilica "in miniature." Look for the Russian influence as S. Clement was exiled to the Crimea to labor in the mines and was bound
to an anchor and thrown in the Black Sea for his missionary work.

The original structure was burned and pillaged by the invading
Normans in 1084. When it was rebuilt in 1857 the builders found
that it had originally rested on an old Roman apartment house a
short distance from the S. Giovanni Laterano church. It was found
to have been a pre-Christian Mithraeum, usually a cave-like place
to worship, for men during the time of Emperor Nero.

*Accessibility: This basilica appears to be a regular place of worship.
Its church on the surface is accessible for wheelchairs. A different story
presents itself at the rear of the interior. A steep set of stairs with good*

handrails takes you down through two levels of Mithraeum caves and possibly a Christian last level that was excavated beneath the Basilica. Not recommended for disabled.

This archeological site covers Roman history from the pre Christian history of Nero's burning of the city in 64 A.D. Excavation has revealed the timbers of houses burnt. Nero is reputed to have played and sang music while he watched the panic-stricken populace flee their burning dwellings.

The next level reveals the remains of a mansion of Titus Flavius Clements who held Christian meetings in secret from the pagan leaders. Clement, a freed Jewish slave of the family, secretly lead this group. After the victory of Constantine's taking of Rome, a Christian church was built being dedicated to Pope St. Clemente in 392 AD.

This church became one of Rome's most popular churches and was visited by the Byzantine Empress Theodora in 548. The Normans invaded the city of Rome in 1084 and laid waste to most of the existing churches including St. Clemente.

The many relics of the past churches were covered up. Later the church was restored in the 18th Century by excavations and rebuilding. This typical mid-level church is now available to view as a remarkable collection of centuries of Roman history. The present day restoration site conducted by the Irish Catholic Church is restoring ancient frescos to add to the other art.

Are these stairs going up or down?

PIAZZA SPAGNA
Spanish steps that lead to a view

SCALINATA DELLA TRINITÀ DEI MONTI-THE SPANISH STEPS

Directions: The Spagna Metro Station delivers you to this neighborhood. The Metro's portal is located to the left of the Spanish Steps on Vicolo del Bottino. It is a walkway that goes next to the Babington Tea Rooms. Self-operated wheelchair lifts and a moving sidewalk takes you an underground to an exit on Viale Trinita dei Monti.

The combination of a small piazza with Fontana della Barcaccia (Fountain of the Ugly Boat), and a French Baroque church, Trinita Dei Monti, at the top of the steps, makes this a favorite tourist sight in Rome. Hundreds of people gather on the steps each day to sit and watch people, take photos of the vista of Rome at the top of the steps, and take photos of the steps. There are horse drawn carriages nearby

The Spagna Steps locate the 19th century fashion and art center of Rome that has been a favorite destination for American and European tourists for two centuries. The Keats-Shelley museum and the Giorgio De Chirico Studio can be found just a few feet from the bottom of the steps. A short walk across the Piazza can take the visitor to Caffé Greco, a coffee house where Casanova once visited makes for Romantic thoughts. Streets that lead from this piazza have some of the most fashionable shops to be found

*Above Keats-Shelley Museum and below Babington's Tea Rooms.
These two buildings flank the Spanish Steps.*

anywhere with their designer labels.

The steps were built in 1725 through funds provided by Etienne Gueffier, a French diplomat. The steep, muddy slopes in front of the French Church/Nunnery, Trinita di Monti, disturbed him. The 137 steps were built surrounded by azalea plants to bridge the popular artistic neighborhood around the boat fountain to the expensive neighborhood at the top of the steep slope.

Accessibility: To reach the top of the steps, it is recommended that you ride the elevator in the Spagna Metro station. Elevators are in the metro to the top of the steps. There are 30 steps from the end of the elevator ride. There is a wheelchair life to bypass those steps if you borrow a key from the tourist office. There also is a ¼ mile moving sidewalk in the metro station that can take you to a sidewalk along the busy road, Viale del Muro Torto, near the Borghese Park entrance.

AT THE TOP
THE TERRACE OF TRINITA DEI MONTI

Today, artists can be seen displaying their works here just as they did during the 19th century. This area around an Egyptian obelisk on the way to the top of the steps is a gathering place for writers, musicians, artists and lovers. The view of the city is excellent from here, however, if one walks to the street Viale Trinita dei Monti. The main door is normally closed; enter through a side door in the convent building. If the door is locked during the normal opening hours, you can ring the bell by the door. Open daily 10 - 1 and 4 – 6:30.

Start strolling down the road to the left and you will find a magnificent view of Rome on the left side and more of the gigantic park of hundreds of acres on the right. If you have time move down this small lane for a little more than a half a mile, you will be at the wonderful Piazza dei Popolo.

If you walk about ¾ of a mile to the northeast across the huge park, you will find the famous Villa Borghese Museum. If you don't feel like walking up to the Borghese Gardens, take the "secret passage" to the Via Veneto. Go into Spagna metro stop, and you'll see a passageway with signs for the Via Veneto. Ride the escalators until you exit at the Via Veneto. Take a left at the old gate, and you'll see the entrance to the Borghese Gardens at Viale S. Paolo del Brasile.

Look around and you will discover the top landing of the elevator that is available at the Spagna Metro Stop. If you don't feel like walking down all the steps take elevator back down to the Metro station.

Sights to see in this area are: Keats-Shelley House Museum; the Giorgio De Chirico Studio; several famous coffee houses; the Villa Borghese Museum; Augustus Mausoleum; the Altar of Peace from the Boat Fountain at the bottom of the steps.

At the Piazza level

KEATS-SHELLEY HOUSE MUSEUM

Piazza di Spagna 26
Tel. 06 6784235
http://www.keats-shelley-house.org
Admission: € 5
Hours: 9 – 1, 3 – 6 Monday - Friday
Directions: The museum is located on the lower right side of the steps.

This is the 18th century house known as Casina Rosa, was occupied by John Keats when he died in 1821 at the age of 25 of tuberculosis. Today it is a working library established in honor of Keats and the poet Percy Shelly. Much memorabilia is shown.

Accessibility: This museum cannot accept wheelchairs.

The Spanish Steps have drawn writers, musicians and artists from all over the world. Poets John Keats and Percy Shelley started this movement in the 1820's when the Steps had just been completed. The museum now contains their works and other writer's such as Byron, George Elliot, Edith Wharton and Oscar Wilde. The coffee house, Antico Caffè Greco built in 1767 still serves the public as it did these artists on the other side of the Piazza Spagna. One can sit at the same table as Oscar Wilde and enjoy a Cappuccino

The love of Rome can be seen in a letter written to Thomas Peacock by Shelley in 1819, "Rome is yet the capital of the world. It is a city of palaces and temples, more glorious than those which any other city contains and of ruins more glorious than they."

CASA-MUSEO GIORGIO DE CHIRICO-GIGIORGIO DE CHIRICO'S STUDI

Piazza di Spagna 31
Tel. 06.679.6546
www.fondazionedechirico.it
Open 10 AM – 1 PM Tuesday – Saturday
Admission: € 5
Directions: It is located on the right side of Keats-Shelley Memorial House

Accessibility: Gallery of 24 pieces of unusual modern art in the former studio of the late artist. An elevator is available after making an appointment for a visit.

Giorgio De Chirico's work is sometimes called a painter of mysticism. This charming private gallery is available for private tours. A telephone speaker is available at the ground floor entrance. A visit demonstrates how an artist can become very successful during his own lifetime and have a place for his own fans to visit.

HONORABLE MENTIONS:
BY THE TIBER

These sights are set next to each other and noted for their early Roman History of the time of Emperor Augustus.

AUGUSTUS MAUSOLEUM - MAUSOLEO AUGUSTO

Via del Corso & Piazza Augusto Imperator

Directions: Walk 5 blocks west towards the Tiber from the Spagna Piazza to reach these sights. Take either Via delle Croce or Via delle Carrozze. This Mausoleum is on Via Ripetta opposite side of the street from the Ara Pacis (Altar of Peace). This looks like a pile of old bricks, it was stripped of its marble facades and surrounding ornamentation by invading barbarians and Romans many centuries ago.

Accessibility: The building area cannot be entered, however the surrounding area, is accessible after climbing 39 steps without handrails. Not recommended for wheelchairs.

This burial place was originally a remarkable circular marble building where the ashes of emperors were kept after Augustus had it built. Its height was 300 feet and it was 150 feet in diameter. A huge bronze statue of Augustus was mounted on a column. Its surrounding structure consisted of concentric circles of concrete with stone marble facing surrounded by circles of tall evergreen trees.

When this mausoleum became overcrowded with burial vases, the Mausoleum of Hadrian was built across the Tiber River near the Vatican. It outlasted this burial place as the present Castle Sant'Angelo. The visitor can only imagine the splendor of both edifices through present day pictures that are available in books by street vendors.

ARA PACIS AUGUSTAE - ALTAR OF PEACE

www.arapacis.it
Address: Lungotevere in Augusta, sited next to the Tiber, across Via di Ripetta from the Mausoleum of Augustus .
Tuesday to Sunday 9:00 AM to 7:00 PM, 24th and 31st December 9:00 AM to 2:00 PM (the ticket office closes an hour in advance) Closed Mondays, January 1st, May 1st and December 25th
Admission: Full price € 6.50 Reductions € 4.50

Directions if you are coming from other areas: Metro red A line: Flaminio exit. Walk through Piazza Del Popolo, and walk down down Via di Ripetta (about 930 yards). Entrance is 150 feet north of where Ponte Cavour crosses Lungotevere in Augusta.

This is an open concrete and glass building located on the eastern bank of the river with easy foot traffic and wheelchair access. The monument inside the building was first built in 13 BC at the order of the Roman Senate. It was built as a hero's welcome to Emperor Augustus for his victories in Spain and Gaul. It first opened in 9 BC.

It was unearthed from the flood plains and moved from an area called the Field of Mars, south from the current location and reconstructed in 1930 to its present location. The pavillion around the monument at that time was soon bunkered for the bombing from WWII and in 1970 the bunker removed and final restoration of the glass pavillion around the mounment was finished.

A number of marble base relief's show many scenes of Augustus family life. A panel shows his family leading a parade to the consecration of a temple. The second panel shows an animal sacrifice and a third shows Agrippa, Caligula and Augustus's scandal ridden daughter Julia.

This is a reconstructed treasure from the time of Augustus. The altar was reconstructed from the fragments scattered in museums for centuries.

VILLA BORGHESE GARDENS-ROME'S CITY PARK

Accessibility: from Line A, Metro station at Spagno and follow signs to exit Muro Torto and Villa Borghese, walk forward for 400 ft. along busy Muro Torto to reach the entrance to Villa Borghese Park and a (600 yards) third of a mile stroll to the Gallery Borghese along Viale del Museo Borghese.

Added features located inside the park: cafes located around the park, 2 and 4-wheeled bike rentals (surreys), tram rides, boat rentals on a beautiful small lake, movie theaters, water clock, lots of benches, wide paved walkways, Wi-Fi access, dog walking, zoo, galleries, villas, children's rides and a place to picnic.

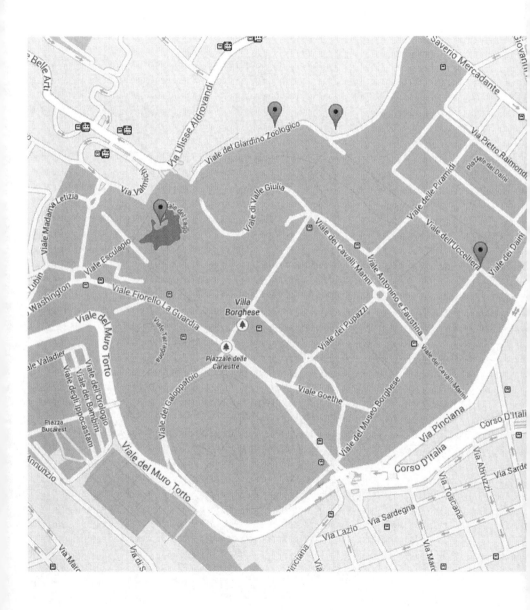

This huge expanse of lawns, statuary and fountains in the city of Rome represents the backyard and garden of all its citizens. When people live in a city, like Rome, they don't have a private yard. This is their "yard" Borghese Gardens more than fulfills this need for the people of Rome. Their pride can be seen in how well they use and maintain this lovely park.

THE HISTORY OF BORGHESE PARK

Cardinal Scipione Borghese, a patron of the artist Bernini, began turning a vineyard into extensive 17 acres of gardens in 1605. In the 19th century the garden's former formality was remade as a landscape garden in an English style. The Villa Borghese gardens were long informally open, but were bought by Rome and given to the public in 1903. The total expanse of the current park is 148 acres and is close in proximity to much of Rome. This is the second largest landscaped park of Rome and contains several villas. The Spanish Steps lead up to this park, The Spagna Metro leads under the hill to the entrance, and there is another entrance at the Porte del Popolo by Piazza del Popolo. The Pincio (the Pincian Hill of ancient Rome), in the south part of the park, offers one of the greatest views over Rome. The leaders of Rome and its people promoted the setting aside of private lands like the Borghese Estate to protect it from land speculation and destruction. Borghese Park represents the work and pressure by the people of Italy to protect their lands and a place to leave beauty for their children

VILLA BORGHESE MUSEUM AND GALLERY-PIAZZA DEL MUSEO BORGHESE

Tel. 06 32810
Reservations **(Required in Advance):** € 2
Admission: € 9
Guided Tours: € 5 + 9
Open: Tuesday to Sunday: 8:30 AM – 6 PM

Self-Guided Tours: Rent the audio headset phone from the gift store, this will give you a private guided tour of what most visitors feel is the greatest museum in Rome.

Admission Policy: There is a policy of limited admissions. Reservations must be made for specific time slots of two and one half hours. There are only 350 admissions at any one time. **You must call in advance or go online to reserve your time slot to visit the gallery ahead of time. Consider 3 days in advance at least.**

www.galleriaborghese.it/borghese/en/evilla.htm

Accessibility: A chairlift is available in the lower floor. The bar, information room, and shops are accessible. The elevator has a doorway wide enough for wheelchairs. Special wheelchairs are available in the lower floor. Special wheelchairs are available for disabled visitors to reach the first floor and shops are accessible. Volunteers also provide escort services.

This museum and gallery is located in the many acres of the Borghese Park. A sign will designate the entrance escalator to the Borghese Gallery. This museum gallery contains classic masterpieces of the 15th to 19th Centuries.

One of the popular pieces is a life-sized nude sculpture of Pauline Bonaparte (sister of Napoleon), by Antonio Canova, in the pose of *Venus Victrix*. The masterpiece Bernini marble sculptures: David and Apollo and Daphne complement the other works. The David is depicted preparing his sling like a baseball pitcher wound up for the pitch. Apollo and Daphne are caught in midair. Daphne is turning into a laurel bush to help her to flee from Apollo's grip. The marble leaves of the bush are carved so thin that if tapped they ring like glass.

The famous painting of *Venus and Cupid with a honeycomb*, 1531, by Cranach, a leading painter of the German Renaissance is said to have the face of his current girlfriend. This was a common practice by artists of this era. This lady with her refined flowing lines is far-removed from the style of ancient statues.

Portrait of a Man, 1475, by Antonello da Messina is breathtaking when you see the use of color for flesh tone and the reds of the robe. This painting could have been done in the 21ˢᵗ century it is so different from the style of the paintings of its era.

The museum is filled with artworks, and frescoed walls and ceilings. This museum is highly recommended and a very popular attraction.

TEMPLE OF ESCALAPIO - LAKE SANTANDER

There is a beautiful lake in the center of the park with the Temple of Escalapio on an island. Boats are available for rent to glide over the lake in this wonderful setting. Watch the ducks frolic around the lake.

The pleasant area of this laghetto can be reached by taking a taxi to Piazza Paolina Borghese. Hikers, joggers, and wheelchairs can move along a path with part asphalt and some graveled hard surface. It is possible to enjoy a stop on Viale del Aranciera at the Casina del Largo, where there is a cafe with outside tables.

CHILDREN'S PARK IN BORGHESE

The park was full of children with their parents having fun. There are a number of children rides running. The laughter from the 4 to 12 year olds watching the traditional Punch & Judy puppet show at the Teatro del Burattino was enjoyable as the parents discreetly watched from nearby benches. The same show they probably enjoyed as children. The Cinema dei Piccoli is a theater that shows children's movies in the afternoon and early evenings. There are vendors with balloons and foods for the families.

You should try to come to this park on a Saturday, Sunday or a National Holiday. I was fortunate to have participated in the Children's Park ritual on Liberation Day on April 25. On that day the entire country celebrates the ending of the German occupation by the Allied Forces. Everything in Rome closes down except the restaurants, transportation system and the parks.

BIOPARCO, GIARDINO ZOOLOGICO BIO PARK AND ROME ZOO

http://www.bioparco.it

Admission: Public events that take place on Saturdays and Sundays are included in the ticket costs.

Adults € 14, Children over 1 meter and under 12 years € 12, Senior citizens 65+ €12, except Wed. € 4

FREE Entry For:children under 3 feet, disabled people, essential caregivers for disabled people

Bioparo Train € 1.50

Check the website above for hours of operation.

By Tram: No. 19 - "Bioparco" stop
By Bus: No. 3 - 52 - 53 - 926 - 217 - 360 - 910
Nearby Stops on the Underground Metro Line A: Piazzale Flaminio, Via Veneto, Spagna
By car: G.R.A. exit "Salaria centro – Parioli"
On foot: Piazzale del Giardino Zoologico No. 1

This modern zoo is a testiment to the care of wild animals. They are very ethical about the animals showing great care about the diets, enviornments and general well-being of the animals. The animals are not on exhibition in cages but set into natural habitats. Many of the animals have come to the zoo because of difficult times from illegal animal trafficking. They are able to do better at the zoo due to their fragmented habitats and poaching in the native areas they came from.

EXPLORA MUSEO DEL BAMBINI DI ROMA THE CHILDREN'S MUSEUM OF ROME-
Admission: € 7
Tel. 06.361.3776

This is a child's size play-town where everything scientific can be observed, touched and experienced. Children are offered the opportunity to discover the mystery of how things function through observation, touch and experiment with help by an adult facilitator. It is similar to the Exploratorium in San Francisco, California.

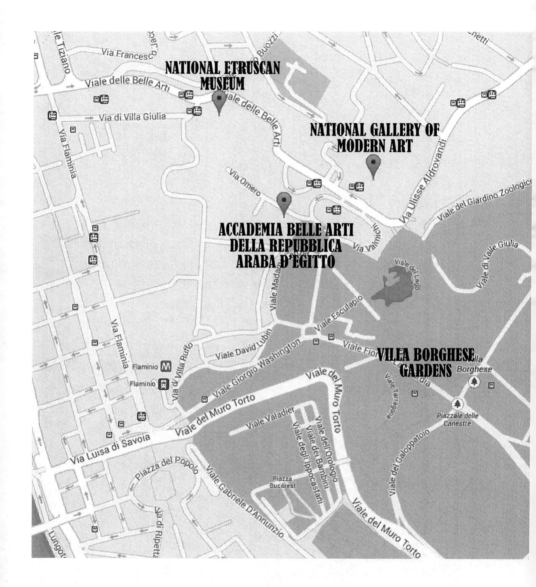

THREE GALLERIES JUST NEXT DOOR TO EACH OTHER

The museums are located just outside the north end of the Borghese Park. It is a 5 minute walk (less than ¼ mile) between the museums on the busy road, Viale delle Belle Arti.

Hint: Take the tram around Rome – Pick up the #3 tram (check website, atac.roma.it) right in front of the National Gallery of Modern Art on Viale delle Belle Arti, for a ride through Rome. A 40 minute ride takes you along the park, through Roman neighborhoods, past ancient walls and aqueducts, right to the Colosseum. You could get off there, or keep on going, past the Circus Maximus, up the Aventine, to Piazza Porta S. Paolo and the Tiber River. (At the Tiber, just get off and take the #3 tram going back to the Villa Borghese Gardens). The tram goes slow, perfect for a Sunday afternoon.

GALLERIA NAZIONALE D'ARTE MODERNA– NATIONAL GALLERY OF MODERN ART

Viale delle Belle Arti, 131
Tel. 06 322981
www.gnam.arti.beniculturali.it/gnamco.htm
Hours: 9 AM to 8 PM, Closed Mondays
Admission: € 7

Accessibility: Indicate to the taxi driver that there is an accessible entrance at Via Gramsci. Elevators and accessible bathrooms are available.

The National Gallery of Modern and Contemporary Art, was established in 1883 with the idea of bringing art to life. This is museum with two souls, as it has two centuries, the nineteenth and twentieth centuries art movements.

The gallery includes one of the greatest collections of paintings and sculptures of artists of the 19th and 20th centuries. It contains artworks by the neo-classicism, romanticism and impression movements. Goya, Delacroix, Blake, Renoir, Rossetti, Courbet, Van Gogh, Degas, Cézanne, Modigliani, Mondrian, Duchamp, de Chirico, Cara, Miro, Kandinsky and Klimt's works are all featured here. Klimt's The Thee Ages and Cézanne's Le Cabanon de Jourdan are worth the trip.

ACCADEMIA BELLE ARTI DELLA REPUBBLICA ARABA D'EGITTO– FINE ARTS ACADEMY OF THE ARAB REPUBLIC OF EGYPT

Via Omero, 4,
+39 06 320 1896
http://www.accademiaegitto.org
(use Google to translate to English)
Library: Mon - Fri: 10 -3 PM

The Academy of Fine Arts of Egypt was conceptualized in 1929 by the Egyptian artist, Ragheb Ayad. He was studying in Italy and wanted to create a bridge of the arts of Egypt in Rome. He sent a letter to the Egyptian government and proposed finding a headquarters for the project and displaying the talents of Egypt's artists. In 1930 the Italian government proposed the donation of a plot of land to build the academy for exchange of land in Cairo to create an institute to house archaeological studies. This seeded many years of planning and in 1961 both countries laid a foundation for this building. In January 1966 was inaugurated.

This building houses an extensive library with a collection of over 10,000 volumes. There are some research volumes and several rare books that show amazing engravings to document the wonders of the world and accomplishments. you can check their library online: http://opac.almavivaitalia.it/IEI/ricercaSemplice.php

Besides painting the Academy also promotes other forms of art by organizing exhibitions of sculpture, photography, performing arts and film and art history in Egypt and Italy. The Gallery also houses the works and experimental productions of the artists participating in the Egyptian State Prize for Artistic Creativity and which are being hosted by the Academy to give them the opportunity to meet and discuss with the Italian culture and present so their works enriched by this multicultural experience.

VILLA GIULIA - MUSEO NAZIONALE ETRUSCO DI VILLA GIULI NATIONAL ETRUSCAN MUSEUM

Piazzale di Villa Giulia, 9

Tel. 06.3226571

Admission: € 5

Hours: 8:30 – 7:30 Tuesday – Sunday

Tram 19

For short walk: leave National Gallery of Modern Art, turn right and head west along Viale delle Belle Arti for 380 yards (approx. ¼ mile) the Etruscan Museum and the National Gallery of Modern Art are both located on the north side of the road and practically next door to each other.

Walking from metro Flamino station: distance .6 of a mile, about 13 minutes. Leave Flamino station, head northeast on Viale David Lubin, road turns left to stay on Viale David Lubin, Turn right onto Via degli Orti Giustiniani, continue straight on Via di Villa Guida for .4 mile, turn left on Viale delle Belle Arti it is 20 yards ahead on the right side of the wide avenue.

Accessibility: Due to the numerous uneven floors, a companion is necessary for any wheelchair visitors. Others should be careful during their movement from one room to another.

The Etruscan fondness for eating and drinking is shown through a number of bronze cooking utensils. A reconstruction of an Etruscan Temple is located in the garden of the Villa another is outdoors.

A precious collection of Etruscan antiquities is on display in this 15th century villa. It was once the home of Pope Julius III. This museum contains most of the few Etruscan works of art remaining from the 7th to 5th centuries BC.

These are just a few of the ones to see:

- The Warrior's Tomb
- An ancient statue of Apollo
- The Sarcophagus of the Spouses
- The tomb of Castro
- The refurbishing of Bernadini of Palestrina
- The refurbishing of Barberini

This is an opportunity to see one of the ancient civilizations before the Roman Empire.

THE POPOLO PIAZZA

Directions: Line A metro station Flamino. Care should be taken in crossing the auto traffic of the Piazza Flaminio. A taxi can provide the safest journey at the heavy traffic time. The Popolo is also available below the south end of Villa Borghese Gardens. There are stairs available to use going down to the piazza.

The Popolo Neighborhood stands at an ancient entrance to Rome. The 13th century BC Egyptian Obelisk of Ramses II was raised and twin churches were added to provide balance to Santa Maria Popolo. Bernini the Sculptor was assigned to place the present elaborate façade on the portico to honor the Queen Christina of Sweden when she converted to Catholicism. Semi-circular walls were built and decorated by 16 marble sphinxes and other statuary. Fountains were built to balance the circular piazza of about ¼ mile in diameter and small flat cobblestones were laid to make it a smooth surface. Restaurants with restrooms, shops and a taxi stand are near the church Santa Maria of the Miracles. It also was a place of pride where the occupying German army left Rome in defeat at the end of World War II.

SANTA MARIA DEL POPOLO-
ST. MARY OF THE PEOPLE

Piazza del Popolo 12

Tel. 06.361.0836

Directions: This church is on your left as you pass through the portico of the Roman City wall from the Flaminio Metro Station. You should visit this church for its famous artworks. It was the first of the churches in the film Angels and Demons.

Accessibility: Not wheelchair accessible. There is a side entrance that is even with the level of the street. Once you are inside, there are eleven steps to climb to a side chapel. A small ramp leads to the flat marble floor of the church. You should exit the church in this same way to avoid the large number of steps in front.

Santa Maria del Popolo was commissioned by Pope Sixtus IV and constructed in 1492. It represents one of the more elegant examples of Early Renaissance Buildings in Rome. Inside there are frescos by Pinturicchio and art by Raphael. There are also two masterpieces by Caravaggio, The Crucifixion of Peter and The Conversion of Paul. A marble skeleton by Bernini stands near the entrance.

The painting of Peter being crucified upside down is a careful presentation of the brutal execution with little apparent emotion. The executioners seem totally detached from the situation. Paul seems to be reeling from their decision to make a comedy out of his request to "Die as the Savior did."

The conversion of St. Paul appears to be a staged presentation of Paul falling off of a huge horse in a stable instead of the religious fall on the road to Damascus. The outstanding nature of these two paintings and Caravaggio's use of light make the visit to this church worthwhile.

THE TWIN CHURCHES

Building for both churches was financed by Cardinal Gastaldi. Carl Rainaldi and Bernini built this churches 1675 – 1679.

SANTA MARIA DEI MIRACOLI - SANTA MARIA CHURCH OF MIRACLES

Via del Corso, 528

Tel. 06 361 0250

Directions: This church is located on the opposite side of the Piazza from Santa Maria Popolo. The other twin church, S. Maria dei Montesanto, next door, is closed. The twin churches face the northern gate of the Aurelian Wall. The churches are called twins because of their similar external appearances but have some differences. The two churches define the three streets that depart the piazza.

Accessibility: The church can be easily entered from the street

The church has a reputation for healing sick and handicapped children. It is an active church today and can be expected to have constant visitation by parents seeking help through prayer for their children.

You will find pictures of children wedged behind all kinds of religious artistry in this church.

SANTA MARIA IN MONTESANTO-SANTA MARIA CHURCH IN HOLY MOUNTAIN

THE CHURCH OF THE ARTISTS
Piazza di Popolo

This is the left church when you face the twins.

It was erected over a church of the same name. Originally by Carlo Rainaldi, the plans were revised by Bernini, and ultimately completed by Carlo Fontana. A belfry was added in the 18th century. The statues of saints on the exterior have been attributed to Bernini's design. The interior has an elliptical plan, with a dodecagonal cupola. In 1825, the church was made a minor basilica.

It was found the church of the artists is built over some interesting tombs. Two pyramid funerary monuments similar to the tomb of Caius Cestius which was at the Vatican and now destroyed. The tombs could have inspired Bernini when he designed the tombs of Agostino and Sigismondo Chigi.

FARTHER AFIELD ACROSS THE TIBER, TRASTEVERE

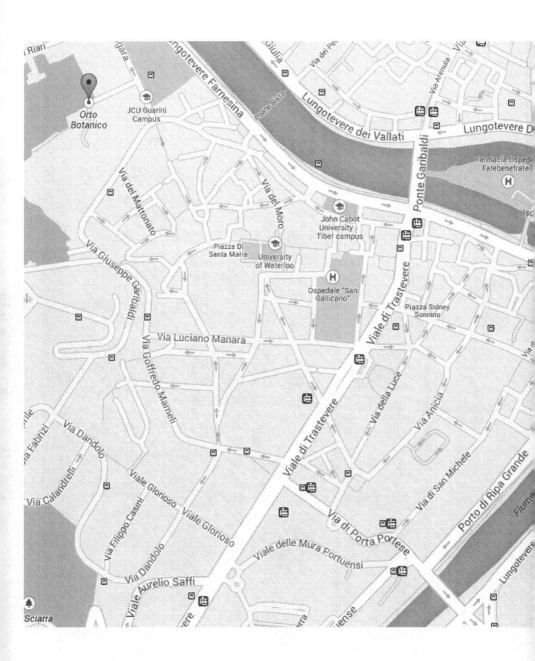

THE PEACEFUL GARDEN DISTRICT ON THE OTHER SIDE OF THE RIVER

The walking district of this garden oriented neighborhood is very charming and intimate. Stroll along the small streets lined in vines, pots of plants and bushes. Get confused by the interconnecting pattern of walkways but keep your eye on the direction of the Tiber and you can always find your way out if you need. Located just south of the Vatican it is filled with small boutiques, cafes, restaurants and musuems, plus the Botanical Garden of Rome, which make this a fine place to visit. Very peaceful and beautiful, that is the Trastevere. Look for small family restaurants with specials handwritten on a board. You will be rewarded.

ST. MARY IN TRASTEVERE

Piazza Santa Maria inTrastevere, 00153 Rome, Italy

06 581 4802

The Basilica of Our Lady in Trastevere is a minor basilica, but one of the oldest churches of Rome, first built around 220. The piazza in front of the church is a favorite to sit around the octagonal fountain and watch people. It is also one of the centers of the local nightlife. The notable beauty of this church is the mosaics, especially the gold tiles in the dome above the front alter. The outside front has found pieces of archeological stone carvings in the wall and mosaics above.

ORTO BOTANICO - BOTANICAL GARDEN

http://sweb01.dbv.uniroma1.it/orto/collezioni.html

Admission: 0-5 yrs free, 6-11 yrs. €4, 12-65 yrs €8, 65+ €4

Take bus 23 or 280, or tram 8

Walk across the Ponte Sisto along via di S. Dorotea, straight on through the Settimiana Gate and a left on the next street via Corsini.

This small garden has the several landscapes of different regions. There is a palm garden with a small fountain and some benches. A favorite for families with small children. They have a garden of roses on the hillside, and if you are able to climb, a view of Rome and the nearby Vatican. The fish pond was small with an interesting herb and medicinals garden. The greenhouses were a little overgrown and some work was needed to bring the garden along. Beautiful bamboo gardens lined some of the paths. There were some large older trees and many strolling paths for a break from the city nearby.

Settimiana Gate

Entrance to the Botanical Gardens

Old bridge across the Tiber

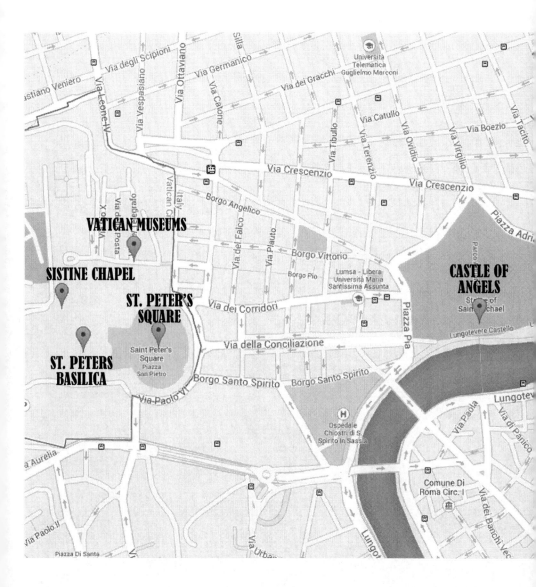

VATICAN, A COUNTRY WITHIN THE CITY OF ROME

The importance of the Vatican with its museums and St. Peter's Basilica cannot be overstated as a place worthy of visitation. Tourists and pilgrims will also find this sight as the most comfortable and accessible place in Rome and should be considered first in time allocation when visiting the city.

The Vatican covers 109 acres of ground, has a 100-man police force, 900 inhabitants, 23 museums and galleries, St. Peter's Basilica, and administrative buildings. But most important, this is the permanent residence of the leader of the Roman Catholics, the Pope.

The Pope and council of Cardinals manages this city/state along with the help of the police force of Swiss guards and a contingent of policemen from the city of Rome. The Swiss are easy to spot in their brightly colored uniforms designed by Michelangelo.

The remarkable history of the Vatican starts at the Circus of Nero, which occupied some of the area of the present St. Peter's Square. It was a place for entertainment with races and commemorative performances, and eventually in 65, a place of Christian martyrdom with the crucifixion of Peter. Finally, this history led to the building of the first 'old' basilica by the first Christian Roman emperor, Constantine in 320.

A Two-Day Visit

Careful scheduling of your time can allow you to visit, if you wish, both the Basilica and 23 museums and galleries in about two days. The necessary elevators, short cuts and resting areas have been located in this guide to make it possible.

Visitors to the Vatican could also visit nearby Castel Sant'Angelo, if you have enough time and ability. This building was an important place of protection for early Popes who needed a safe haven from the many invasions of foreign armies and mobs after the Empire fell apart. Today it is a place to climb through the dark winding interior passage and see a good view of Rome. The dome at St. Peter's Balsilica also has a great view.

PIAZZA DI SAN PIETRO - ST. PETER'S SQUARE

The piazza leads up to one of the most important Catholic cathedrals, St. Peter's. The piazza started in 1656, with its dramatic ellipsoidal colonnade was designed and built in 21 years by Gian Lorenzo Bernin. This large "square" can become a gathering place for thousands of pilgrims, tourists, priests and nuns expressing their admiration and allegiance to the Pope.

SUGGESTIONS FOR CATHOLICS VISITING THE VATICAN:

Use the following information to schedule the places and people you want to see. For example, you can schedule a public audience with the Pope by calling 06.6988.3114 from your hotel. If you wish a private audience, it can be obtained in advance through your local Bishop before you leave home. You are encouraged to see the places in the directory. You are here; make the most of this wonderful opportunity.

VATICAN DIRECTORY

VATICAN TOURIST INFORMATION

The office is located on the left of St. Peter's square as you face the Basilica.

Telephone: 06.6988.1662

Via dell' Umiltá 30, Rome

www.vatican.va

Open 8:30 AM – 6:30 PM, Monday – Saturday.

DRESS CODE

The Vatican enforces a dress code in St. Peters Basilica and the Vatican Museums. This applies to shorts, mini-skirts, sleeveless shirts and bare shoulders. A light sweater in summer is particularly valuable to carry anywhere in Rome when entering churches or Cathedrals.

AUDIENCES WITH THE POPE

Sundays: The Pope addresses the crowd in St. Peter's Square at noon when he is in Rome. Admission and access is free.

Wednesday 10:00 a.m. in the summer and 10:30 a.m. in the winter, The Pope holds a general audience in the morning in the Square. If the weather is inclement he meets in Sala Nevi Audience Hall. Those needing free tickets for his audience should apply to Prefettura della Casa Pontificia 06.6988.3114, 6988.3273, Fax: 06.6988.5863,

Open 9:00 a.m. – 1:30 p.m. Monday – Saturday. Tickets should be picked up on the morning of the audience at the guarded bronze door, just to the left of the Basilica.

For a private audience, your local bishop has to make a written request, which can take between three months and a year to be granted.

SAN PIETRO BASILICA-
ST. PETER'S BASILICA

Tel: 06.6988.1662

Open: 7 AM - 6 PM

Closed for Pontifical Services.

Admission: Free, audio guide available for €6 at cloakroom after security check.

THE DOME

Climbing or riding an elevator to the first level reaches the inside of the dome.

Open: April –September 8 AM – 6 PM. October – March 8 AM – 5 PM

Admission: €4.13 Lift or €3.62 Stairs.

Tel: 06.6988 1662

CUPOLA (TOP OF THE DOME)

Enter tunnel entrance on one side of the dome's first level. Be prepared to climb 320 marble steps to the highest view in Rome.

Special Note: No one will be allowed access to the dome if the Pope is giving mass at the cathedral that day.

THE VATICAN GARDENS

The gardens can be visited on guided tours aboard a minibus that moves through the Pope's back yard. Tours take place on Tuesday, Thursday and Saturday, in good weather.

Information: 06.6988.4676 or tours one week in advance

Admission: €12

TOMBS OF THE POPES

This special tour, under the Basilica, requires a permit obtained at least a day in advance from the Vigilanza Della Citta del Vaticano, office of the guards.

Reservations: Tel: 06.6988 3023.

Accessibility. You may leave by using three steps at the exit of the Tombs. Note: it is best for disabled visitors to return to the entrance level and exit at this point.

Two hundred and sixty-two (262) Popes led the Roman Catholic Church from Peter's delegation by Christ, "you are Peter, and upon this rock I will build this church." Doctrine, churches and the artistic leadership of buildings in Rome depended upon the spiritual inspiration and skill of each of the popes. From Emperor Constantine's time to the present, they resided in various parts of Rome and France. Their present residence in the Vatican seems to have remained the symbolic center of the church because of Peter's crucifixion at that location, which throughout history has lead pilgrims flocking to the tomb of the founder of the Roman Church.

The Vatican City is one of the smallest independent countries in the world. It has its own radio and television station, railway station, supermarket, heliport, diplomatic service, postal service and Swiss Army Guard. It also has its own stamps, currency, the world's finest collection of art and an observer to the United Nations in New York City.

In 1506 the weakened 1,000-year-old basilica was torn down under the leadership of Pope Julius. In 1547 Michelangelo led the construction of the church. Before his death in 1564 at 87, Michelangelo developed the plan for the present immense dome. This world's largest brick dome was completed in 1590. Carlo Maderno put up the new façade topped by huge statues of Christ and the Apostles. Bernini finished St. Peter's square with the elliptical piazza by 1667 with a 289 column, 88-pillar colonnade crowned with 140 statues of saints.

THE FLOOR PLAN OF ST. PETER'S BASILICA

Reservations: Admission is free except for special tours. Reservations should always be made for these special tours since the lines can be quite long and tiresome.

Tel: 06.69885318

Transportation: metro line A gets the visitor to the Vatican through the Ottaviano-SanPietro Station. You will need to walk about 900 yards to the entrance of St. Peter's Basilica. The Basilica entrance is about 500 steps from the Vatican taxi stand.

Tel. Piazza San Pietro 06.69884466

Entrance Accessibility; Wheelchairs and interested tourists should enter on the right side of the Basilica at Porta Sobieski. There is an elevator that bypasses 25 steps at the entrance. The interior of the Basilica is totally accessible.

Restroom Accessibility; They are located back toward the center of the outside colonnade.

Entering the interior of St.Peter's Basilica

The Porta Sobieski elevator takes you to the interior of the Basilica. You now have access to an extremely large number of important sights within the Basilica.

Tour of the Terrace on the Roof

Accessibility: Ride to the top of the Basilica by riding an elevator that is about 25 feet from the elevator at the entrance. Paying €5 and riding the elevator can get you to the terrace quickly. This will also get you to a point whereyou can enterior the interior of the dome.

Many statues of saints are at the top of the façade and can be seen up close. An excellent view of the city of Rome is well worth the trip for picture taking. Restrooms, postage stamps, and souvenirs are also available.

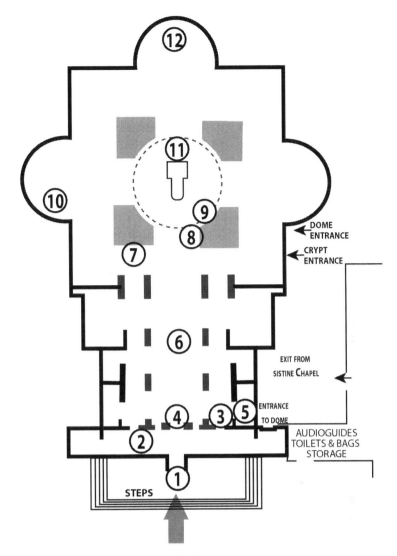

ST. PETER'S SQUARE

1. ENTRANCE
2. ATRIUM
3. HOLY DOOR
4. CENTRAL DOOR
5. PIETA BY MICHELANGELO
6. PIETA CHAPEL
7. ALTAR OF TRANSFIGURATION BY RAFAEL
8. STATUE OF ST. PETER
9. ENTRANCE TO THE VATICAN GROTTOS
10. SITE OF ST. PETER'S CRUCIFIXION
11. CONFESSION AND PAPAL ALTAR
12. THRONE OF ST. PETER IN GLORY
    OR CATTEDRA BY BERNINI

FLOOR PLAN OF ST. PETER'S BASILICA

THE TOUR OF THE DOME

Visitors wishing to view the interior of the dome should be prepared to climb 22 metal steps through a passageway from the terrace to the inside of the dome. You should consider climbing to this wonderful interior view of the Basilica. However, wheelchairs will not be able to enter this area. Walking around the interior of the dome may lead you to be tempted to climb to the Cupola on the top of the dome. Be aware, you will be climbing up a very narrow stairway of about 200 stone steps that could cause some extreme fatigue. Unfortunately this is a situation where once you start up you cannot change your mind because of all the people who are behind you.

However, if you make the climb to the cupola, you will be rewarded with fantastic 360° view of the city of Rome and the buildings and grounds of the Vatican.

Castel Sant'Angelo, the Pope's haven during ancient warfare can easily be reached by walking down Via Dei Corridor from the front of St Peter's. Vatican entrance can be reached by following the flat and passable Via de Porta Angelica along the wall of the Vatican from the left side of St. Peters.

If you wish you can choose to see the Castel Sant'Angelo before you go to see the museums.

Vatican Museums & Galleries

People gather in the courtyard to enter the many entrances to the museums housed at the Vatican. This modern metal sculpture that slowly spins is named, Sphere within a Sphere, by Arnaldo Pomodoro.

MUSEO VATICANO-
VATICAN MUSEUMS

Website with interactive map:
http://saintpetersbasilica.org/vaticancity-map.htm
Admission:
March - October, Monday – Friday 8:45 AM 5:45 PM
November – February, Monday – Friday 8:45 AM 1:45 PM
Closed on major religious holidays
Admission: €10
Audio guides are available: €10
Tel. 06.6988.3333 or 1662 Fax: 06.6988.5061

Some consider this collection of museums and galleries to be some of the most important art collections in the world. In addition to the museums it also comprises a great complex of the Apostolic Palaces consisting of galleries, frescoed rooms, the Sistine Chapel, the Chapel of Nicholas V and many rooms of paintings by Raphael. There are over 60,000 priceless art pieces displayed in 1,407 rooms.

Accessibility: The best time of the day to begin your visit is often at noon. It is always packed with visitors and the tours are often a little thinner at this time. This is not to say, the musuems will be not packed, they will be. Wheelchair and tired tourists should take a taxi from the Castle Sant' Angelo or the Piazza St. Peters. The taxi stop is near a small cobblestone piazza off a very busy street called Viale Vaticano. metro train A Ottaviano/San Pietro station is the nearest metro stop. It is recommend that metro riders take the taxi to the museums' entrance.

There are resting places, a cafeteria, a coffee shop and a number of comfortable benches. There is a bathroom equipped for the disabled in the Museo Gregorian Profano adjacent to the entrance (ask an attendant). All attendants are very helpful and they speak English. It is possible to use museum wheelchairs by telephoning at least 24 hours in advance 06.69883860. Seniors or wheelchair visitors wishing to use the three special itineraries for the handicapped should have at least one member of their party schedule a wheelchair. It will give you entry to special help.

ENTRANCES & EXITS

There is usually a long line to enter the main entrance of the museums. You may not want to climb the 44 stone stops to get to where you can purchase your tickets. Ask an attendant to take you up in the elevator to bypass this climb. Remember, this entrance is built on the side of a hill and you should take full advantage of the elevators. Once you have paid €10 for your tickets, you face a spiral ramp of 5 turns, which is far too steep for anyone pushing a wheelchair. Take the elevator up past this ramp if you are a wheelchair rider. If you are not in a wheelchair, you could instead try the long escalator.

Once you have put your ticket through the subway style turnstile, it is suggested that you call for the 3rd elevator, unless you feel like climbing 13 more stone steps. This brings you up to the large circular balcony Cortile delle Corazze, which gives you access to the Vatican Post Office, a wonderful cafeteria, money exchange, shops and more bathrooms.

It would be a good idea at this point to sit down with your guidebook to decide what you want to see and how much time you want to spend. To avoid the next 50 steps you should take a 4th elevator up to the first floor of the museum. Do not be shy asking for this service. Just ask for the "lift" or the ascensore (a-sen-so-rey).

REGULAR ITINERY OF THE MUSEUMS & GALLERIES

(Use Guide to the Vatican Museum, Vatican Press, €9 for details)

FLOOR #1

- Egyptian Museum (Museo Egizio) 10 rooms of bas-relief's & statues.
- Chiaramonti Museum (Museo Chiaramonti) Nearly 1,000 pieces of classical sculpture, at end of museum turn right before Lapidary door.
- Braccio Nuovo Statues & Mosaics, (retrace steps to start of

Chiaramonti Museum).
- Pio Clementine Museum 12 rooms Greek/Roman statues, busts & muses.

CLIMB STAIRS
FLOOR #2

- Etruscan Museum, 19 rooms of sarcophagi, tombs, bronzes & jewelry
- Room of the Biga (chariot) statuary above Atrium of the Four Gates
- Gallery of Candelabra, 300 BC to 200 AD frescoes, sarcophagi & statues
- Gallery of Tapestries, 16th & 17th century Flemish tapestries

Elevator is here for returning to 1st floor library for a shortcut to the Sistine Chapel

- Gallery of Maps, Forty 16th Century maps & elaborate ceilings
- Apartment of Pius V tapestries & friezes from 15th & 16th centuries
- Sobieski Room & Immaculate Conception large paintings
- Raphael Room many paintings by Raphael, Loggia of Raphael
- (Scholars only) Room of the Chiaroscuri "Secret" of the Cardinals Chapel of Nicholas V 13th Century tower chapel room.

Return to lower first floor by steps

Mosaic floor in heavy use at the Vatican. Part of the art that surrounds you

Some examples of the
Statues at the musuems.

Above, map detail, in Gallery of the maps hallway. Below ceiling mosaic detail in Popes Rooms.

Detail of tapestry from the Gallery of the Tapestries.
This tells the story of the killing of the
male infants.

VATICAN MUSEUMS

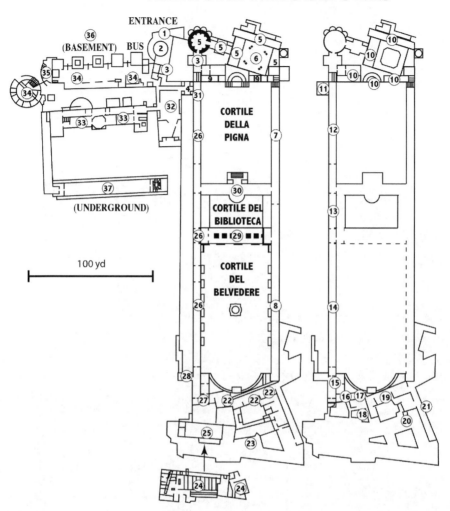

ENTRANCE

(BASEMENT) BUS

CORTILE DELLA PIGNA

CORTILE DEL BIBLIOTECA

CORTILE DEL BELVEDERE

(UNDERGROUND)

100 yd

1. Elevator
2. Stairs
3 Vestibule (tickets, information)
4. Atrium of the Four Gates
5. Pio-Clementine Museum
6. Cortile Ottagono
7. Chiaromonti Museum
8. Lapidary Gallery
9. Museo Gregoriano Egizio
   (Egyptian Museum)
10. Museo Gregoriano Etrusco
    (Etruscan Museum)
11. The Biga Room (chariot)
12. Gallery of the Candelabra
13. Galleria degli Arazzi
    (Tapestry Gallery)

14. Galleria delle Carte
    Geografiche (Map Gallery)
15. Pius V's Chapel
16. Sobieski Room
17. The Immaculate Conception Room
18. Urban VIII's Chapel
19. Raphael's rooms
20 Nicholas V's Chapel
21. Logge di Raffaello
    (Loggias of Raphael)
22. Borgia Apartment
23. Borgia Rooms
24 Collezione d'Arte Religiosa Moderna
    (Museum of Modern Religious Art)
25. Sistine Chapel
26. Vatican Library

27. Museo Sacro della Biblioteca
28. Sala delle Nozze Aldobrandine
    (Room of the Aldobrandini Wedding)
29. Salone Sistino (part of library)
30. New Wing
31. Museo Profano della Biblioteca
32. Cortile della Pinacoteca (courtyard)
33. Pinacoteca (Picture Gallery)
34. Museo Gregorian Profano
    (Museum of Secular Art)
35. Pio Cristiano Museum
36. Missionary-Ethnological Museum
37. Museo Storico (Historical
    Museum)

FLOOR #1
Borgia Apartments 28 rooms of modern art

Walk down 60 steps to entrance of Sistine Chapel. Wheelchair & seniors go to Vatican library & enter Sistine exit.

Sistine Chapel Michelangelo's fresco masterpieces

Exit out passageway containing 8 steps & wheelchair lift to make this the entrance for wheelchairs.

FLOOR #1
Vatican Libraries long hallways containing furniture & manuscripts

Walk to the Vestibule of Four Gates & the Pinacoteca Court for bathrooms, cafeteria & gift shops. Elevators are available for exiting museums. Those continuing, go to Pinacoteca.

Pinacoteca, 15 rooms of paintings & tapestries from 11th to 19th centuries.

Gregorian Profane Museum 5 sections of marble pieces

Pio Christian Museum Early Christian sarcophagi & mosaics.

Missionary –Ethnological Museum 99 exhibits from foreign missions.

Carriage Museum 21 exhibits of Papal carriages & cars.

Return to Courtyard of the Pinacoteca to exit museums through elevators from the circular balcony.

Remember, this is the total tour and flow of traffic. I do not recommend this for wheelchairs or tired tourists in one day. Examine the following itineraries or the ones recommended in the Vatican guide book and decide which ones fit your schedule.

SPECIAL ITINERARIES FOR SENIORS & WHEELCHAIRS

Attendants should be contacted for assistance on these tours when entering the main entrance. Individuals in wheelchairs will have no problem getting assistance. However, seniors must make it clear they have endurance problems and would appreciate taking these special routes that mainly lead to a different approach to the Sistine Chapel.

The Roman Social Service Organization recommends that fragile seniors and disabled visitors choose from one of these three Special Itineraries. These itineraries were designed for an easier journey through selected museums. They are different than the standard tour in the following ways:

• Visitors move in a different direction
• Certain exhibits are be passed to avoid long stair ways and irregular floors
• Time is shortened for the comfort of the visitor.

If you choose to have a special itinerary ask an attendant at the entrance for "special itinerary for disabled visitors". (Speciale Itinerario per Turista Anziano e Disable). Show them the itinerary in my book and you will be scheduled for assistance. You may ask for the loan of a wheelchair at that time.

ITINERARY #1
Sistine Chapel & Vatican Library
Time: 1-Hour First Floor

Ground floor – Entrance – Show the Itinerary to one of the helpful attendants.
1. Circular Balcony Cortile della Corazze
2. Atrium of the Four Gates Atrio delle Quattro Cancelli
3. Vatican Library Gallaerie della Biblioteca Apoltolica Vaticana.
 You must travel against the regular flow of visitor traffic.

Sign in courtyard describing the details of the Sistine Chapel's ceiling.

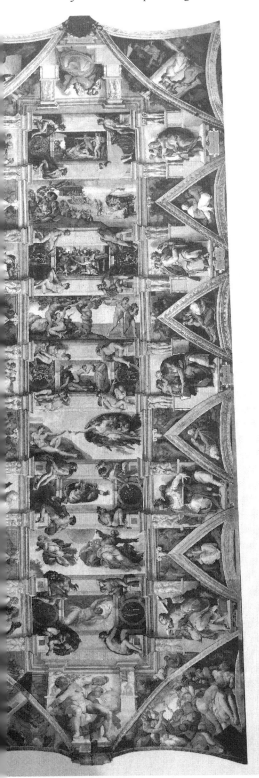

MICHELANGELO
CREAZIONE DI ADAMO - CREATION OF ADAM

MICHELANGELO
PROFETA GEREMIA - PROPHET JEREMIAH

MICHELANGELO
SIBILLA DELFICA - DELPHIAN SIBYL

MICHELANGELO
LUNETTA DI AZOR E SADOCH PRIMA E DOPO IL RESTAURO
LUNETTE WHIT AZOR, ZADOCH BEFORE AND AFTER THE CLEANING

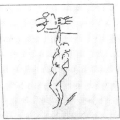

MICHELANGELO
SCHIZZO DELL'ARTISTA AL LAVORO
SULLA VOLTA DELLA CAPPELLA SISTINA
SKETCH OF THE ARTIST WORKING
ON THE CEILING OF THE SISTINE CHAPEL

MICHELANGELO
SCHIZZO DELLA SEZIONE DE
DELLA CAPPELLA SISTINA
SKETCH OF THE SECTION ON
SCAFFOLDING OF THE SISTIN

RESTAURATORE ALL'OPERA
RESTORER AT WORK

CREAZIONE DELL'UOMO, PARTICOLARE
CREATION OF MAN, DETAIL DURING TH

Sistine Chapel　Michelangelo's famous masterpieces

To avoid stepping the approximately 30 steps down to the entrance ask for the exit tunnel of the chapel.

The attendants will guide you to the end of the library galleries, there is the exit from the Sistine Chapel and become your entrance and exit. A wheelchair lift run by attendants lowers wheelchairs over the 8 steps in the tunnel. The attendant will need to halt exiting visitors for you to enter.

Expect to see a large group looking at the wonderful frescoes in the chapel. Wheelchairs can go within about 20 steps of the altar. Four steps block complete movement to the altar. A number of benches are present for resting and gazing at the walls and ceilings. There is no time limit in the chapel. An attendant will operate the chair lift for wheelchairs. Your Silence is Appreciated! The 3rd Itinerary has several extra pages of a poem written by Michelangelo complaining about the pains of painting the ceiling for four years. That and some special information about the chapel are there.

Vatican Library

You are now going with the flow of visitors. Take your time on your way to the museum exit.

Atrium of the Four Gates

Circular Balcony Bathrooms, post office, shops and the cafeteria are here take an elevator to the museum Ground Floor Exit. Accessible bathroom is available in Museo Gregoriano Profano.

ITINERARY #2

Pio Clementine Museum, Egyptian Museum, Vatican Library & Sistine Chapel

Time: 2 hours- First Floor.(Show itinerary to one of the helpful attendants)

1.　circular balcony Cortile della Cancelli,

2. Pio Clementine Museum rooms of animals, muses, rotunda & Greek Cross.
3. Ask attendant for access to Egyptian Museum
4. Egyptian Museum
5. Pio Clementine Museum Cabinet of Apoxyomenos, Octagonal Court, Gallery of statues & Room of busts.
6. Atrium of the Four Gates
7. Vatican Library Gallerie della Biblioteca Apoltolica Vaticana (You must travel against the flow of regular visitors.)

Sistine Chapel

To avoid having to walk down about 30 large steps to the entrance of the chapel ask the attendants to guide you to the chapel's EXIT tunnel. The exit from the Sistine Chapel will become both your entrance and exit.

A chair lift run by attendants will lower wheelchairs over the 8 steps in the tunnel. The attendant will need to halt exiting visitors for you to enter.

Expect to see large crowds to be looking at Michelangelo's frescoes. Wheelchairs can go to within about 20 paces of the altar. Four steps block complete movement to the altar. Four steps block complete movement to the altar. A number of benches are present for resting and gazing at the frescoed walls and ceilings. There is no time limit for the chapel. However, visitors are asked to maintain a respectful silence. Leave by going out the exit that you entered. An attendant will operate chair lift. The 3rd Itinerary has some verses of a poem written by Michelangelo about the pains of painting the ceiling for 4 years. Some other information is also available.

Atrium of the Four Gates

Circular Balcony Bathrooms, post office, shops & cafeteria are here. An elevator is available to the museum ground floor exit. Accessible bathrooms available in Museo Gregoriano Profano.

ITINERARY #3

Vatican Library, Gallery of the Tapestries, Gallery of Maps, Apartment of St. Pius V, Rooms of Sobieski, Immaculate Conception, Raphael, Incendio, Segnatora, Heliodorus, Constantine, Chiaroscuri, Chapel of the Beato Angelico and Sistine Chapel

Time: 2-1/2 Hours First & Second Floors. Show itinerary to one of the helpful Attendants.

1. First Floor Circular Balcony Cortile delle Corazze
2. Atrium of the Four Gates Atrio delle Quattro Cancelli
3. Vatican Library Gallerie dell Biblioteca Apostica Vaticana. You must travel against the flow of regular visitors. Take an elevator (lift) in Room III of the library to the floor above.
4. Second floor, Gallery of the Tapestries- Galleria degli Arazzi
5. Gallery of Maps -Galleria delle Carte Geografiche
6. Apartment of St. Pius V Galleria e Cappella de S. Pio V.
7. Sobieski Room Sala Sobieski
8. Immaculate Conception Room Sala dell'Immaculata
9. Raphael Room's Stanze de Raffaello Non-Accessible bathroom is available
10. Incendio Room's Stanze dell'Incendio
11. Seginatora Room's
12. Heliodorus Room Stanze de Eliodoro
13. Constantine Room
14. Chiaroscur Room
15. Chapel of the Beato Angelico

Return through the Rooms Stanza dell'Incendio. Ask the Attendant to open the gate and show you the route back. At the Apartment of Sant Pio V turn right to the elevator. Take the lift down and turn left on arrival at the Vatican Library first floor. You are once again moving against the regular flow of museum visitors.

SISTINE CHAPEL

At the end of the library galleries there is the exit from the Sistine Chapel. A chair lift run by attendants lowers wheelchairs over the 8 steps in the tunnel. The attendant will halt exiting visitors.

Expect a large group looking at Michelangelo's frescoes. Wheelchairs can go within about 20 paces of the altar. Four steps block complete movement to the altar in a wheelchair.

A number of benches are present for resting and gazing at the artwork on the walls and ceilings. There is no time limit for the chapel. Leave through the exit that you entered. Attendants will operate chair lift for wheelchairs.

MICHELANGELO AND THE SISTINE CHAPEL

The Sistine Chapel in which Michelangelo worked for the best part of four years, is a simple rectangular building with frescoed ceilings and walls. Work began in 1476. The Sistine Chapel became the principal place of worship for the Papal "Chapel" , a corporation body consisting of the pope and about two hundred officials in the Vatican.

As well as serving as a place of worship, the chapel houses the cardinals during the conclave when the new pope is elected. Conclaves last several days and nights during which the cardinals camp in the Chapel in temporary cells erected for the purpose. A temporary chimney is added to the side of the chapel for the purpose of the cardinals burning the paper or paper and straw showing their decision. White smoke means they elected a new pope, black smoke means they have not come to a majority decision.

Its dimensions are those of Solomon's Temple, as they are describe in the Book of Kings. It's length is twice it's height and three times it's width. The surfaces of Solomon's Temple were covered in cedar and gold, but the Sistine Chapel was intended from the outset to be decorated with paintings. Pope Sixtus IV had commissioned leading artists of the time, including Perugino, Signoselli and Botticelli to paint two continuous fresco cycles on its walls. On one of the chapel's long walls, they painted scenes from the life of Christ; on the other, scenes from the life of Moses. The meaning of this parallelism is underscored by inscriptions on the cornice declaring that Moses to whom God gave the Ten Commandments, 'is the bearer of the Old Law', while Christ is 'the bearer of the New Law'.

Michelangelo was summoned by Pope Julius II to paint the chapel. The artist felt he was more of a sculptor than a painter, but the Pope insisted and promised that Michelangelo would be in charge of the project. The artist had primarily been a sculptor and had not experience with painting frescos.

So he hired Florentine artists who were trained in frescos and got them working on his plans. He would study them at work and learn from them. Eventually, he learned enough that one day they went to lunch and he locked them out. Without a word, he destroyed their work and started painting the entire ceiling himself. The angry Florentine artists eventually gave up and went back to Florence. Michelangelo painted and re-painted several sections because the work required that he find an appropriate sizing to his characters while standing from the distance of the floor.

Noah's drunkenness portrayal on the ceiling

If you look at the scene of the Drunkenness of Noah where his sons demonstrate their shame of their father, the artist expressed how he felt that the sons were hypocrites. Although Michelangelo was an inexperienced painter, he shows that he was a theologian.

He could also express himself as a poet through the following verses. Michelangelo wrote a comical poem about the experience, which he dedicated to a friend, Giovanni from Pistola, who is unknown;

I've got myself a goiter from this strain,
As water gives the cats in Lombardy
Or maybe it is in some other countries;
My belly's pushed by forced beneath my chin.

My beard toward Heaven, I feel the back of my brain
Upon my neck, I grow the breast of a Harpy,
My brush, above my face continually,
Makes it a splendid floor by dripping down.

My loins have penetrated to my paunch,
My rump's a crupper, as a counterweight,
And pointless the unseeing steps I go.
In front of me my skin is being stretched

While it folds up behind and forms a knot,
And I am bending like a Syrian bow.
And judgment, hence, must grow,
Borne in the mind, peculiar and untrue;

You cannot shoot well when the gun's askew.
John, come to the rescue
Of my dead painting now, and of my honor;
I'm not in a good place, and I'm no painter.

Author's comment— "The Vatican is one of my favorite places to be inspired. I love the sprit of the visitors. When I see Mexican friends coming to the Pope's appearances in their China Poblanas cheering, "Viva Papa!" I get misty-eyed in spite of the fact that I'm a member of the Unity Church."

HADRIAN'S MAUSOLEUM-CASTEL SANT' ANGELO

Address: Lungotevere Castello 50
Tel. 06.689111
Admission: € 5 free for under 18 or over 50.
Hours: 9 AM – 7 PM

Accessibility: A chair lift is available for access to the basement floor. There is a large elevator for the 1st and 2nd floor, which can be used by disable and senior tourists. Staff is available to assist on the 1st and 2nd floors.

Location: Six blocks from Piazza San Pietro down Via dei Corridori to the river.

Via dei Corridori can offer a relaxing walk to Saint Angelo. Venders set up a fine display of goods ranging from handbags to food, offering a diversion before you enter the Castle.

Emperor Hadrian built this mausoleum which is near of the present day Vatican. The mausoleum was built in 123 A.D. Emperor Aurelain fortified the building when he built the city wall in about 275 A.D. It was further fortified when it became a residence and refuge for the Popes whenever enemy armies besieged the city of Rome. The popes converted the structure into a castle, beginning in the 14th century; Pope Nicholas III connected the castle to St. Peter's Basilica by a covered fortified corridor called the Passetto di Borgo.

The courtyard and terrace are inaccessible because of the many stairs. For those able to make the climb, a vista deck and cafe are on the top floor with tables giving fantastic views across Rome.

Special features around the mausolem give this site a commanding presence. In 1669 Pope Clement IX commissioned Bernini's studio to produce 10 angels holding instruments of the passion which now decorate the bridge. Ponte Sant'Angelo is a formal footpath entrance crossing the Tiber to the mausoleum. At the top of the mausoleum, a catapult with a pile of large round stones can be seen, look up and you can then see, close-up, the statue of Archangel Michael erected after a legend that an angel appeared on the roof of the castle to announce the end of the plague. This is why the location was renamed Castel Sant'Angelo from Hadrian's Mausoleum.

If you plan on visiting the 23 museums and galleries of the Vatican ,walk back on Via dei Corridori; turn right at Via di Porta Angelica and follow the crowds down Viale Bastion di Michelangelo. If you plan that experience for another day get a cab to your hotel, or use the metro, Ottaviano-SPietro Station

View across Rome from the top of Castel Sant' Angelo. Well worth the climb but you have to be in good shape to climb all the steep ramps and narrow steps. This is not recommended for disabled people.
The Vittorio Monument is below, flanked with its chariot riders as it sits above the rest of Rome on the Capitoline Hill.

Special Feature

World War II, Rome & Italy
HONORING AMERICAN SERVICEMEN

Via Rasella (The Sad Street)
World War II Historical Notation
A Loyola Rome Student's Guide to World War II in Rome & Italy
By: Philip R. O'Connor, PhD, of Chicago

"In the late afternoon of March 23, 1944, a 156 man contingent of the German 'Bolzano' Police unit marched three abreast up the Via Rasella towards the intersection with the Via della Quattro Fontane, near the Quirinal Palace. These police were men considered too old for front line duty but were favored by the German high command.

Via Rasella runs roughly parallel to Via del Tritone that lies to the west. As the lead rank of the column of singing Tyroleans, reached the top of the street at the Palazzo Tittoni, a powerful bomb was detonated. Twenty-six Bozen men were killed and seven more were dead of injuries by the next morning."

The German Gestapo killed 335 Roman citizens in retaliation within a week. This atrocity was described in a 1980's movie, Morte di Roma (Death in Rome) with Richard Burton playing the commander of the Gestapo in Rome.

Nothing of this action can be seen today, but the street Via Rasella, shows some results of the explosion and is referred to as a "sad street" by modern Romans.

VISITING MEMORIALS TO AMERICAN SERVICEMEN.

MEMORIES OF WORLD WAR II IN ITALY

Seniors who fought in Italy and/or their families have asked for directions to find war memorials while they are visiting Rome. A friend of the author's, Philip R. O'Connor, Ph.D. of Chicago wrote a 44 page book, A LOYOLA ROME STUDENT'S GUIDE TO WORLD WAR II IN ROME AND ITALY. He was kind enough to allow utilization of the information he gathered in this valuable document. Excerpts from this book are shown in the next several pages within "quotation marks". Dr. O'Connor was also kind enough to allow readers of this book to download his book on their computer Acrobat Program, at no cost by e-mailing him at Phil.Oconnor@constellation.com or PhilOconnor@earthlink.net We are indebted to him for this important information and offer.

THE SECRET ARMISTICE

Successful action by the Allies early in the war in Sicily led to a secret planned Armistice between representatives of the King of Italy and the Allies in 1943. In essence, Italy agreed to join the Allies in their campaign to defeat Germany and drive them out of Italy. This planned armistice was a signal to Germany to rush many of their troops to occupy all of Italy to protect their own southern borders.

THE WAR OF LIBERATION

This series of battles required the bloodshed of about 350,000 Italian civilians and thousands of Italian soldiers who fought along side the Allies. The cost of this two-year battle was over 114,000 American casualties of which 29,000 were killed or declared missing. Thousands of English, French, and German soldiers also died during these battles. Large parts of Italy south of Rome were heavily damaged, particularly in the city of Naples. The city of Rome was spared a great deal of damage by a joint proclamation as an Open City.

Locating War Memorials

"Be on the lookout in town and village piazzas and churches through out Italy for plaques and other memorials to the experience of the war. Tip-off Italian words, in addition to the date on the **lapide** (plaque) to look for are **caduta** (the fallen**), Guerra mondiale** (world war), **resistenza** (resistance), **partigiano** (partisans), **soldato** (soldiers), **tedesco** (German), **alleato** (Allies) and **patria** (fatherland).

"Safe Houses in Rome"

There were places in Rome where escaped Allied Prisoners, Italian Jews and partisans hid from the Germans during the occupation. At times these "safe houses", through the courage of their owners, hid as many as several thousand people all over Rome at any one time. Dr. O'Connor has identified some of these and described their locations; .

- "Vicolo Domenico Cellini (directly across Corso Vittorio Emanuele from the Chiesa Nuova);
- Via Firenze (near the Piazza della Repubblica)
- The North American College, a seminary mainly for U.S. and Canadian Seminarians (as well as a few German and Japanese students) in Via del Gianicolo at the base of the Janiculum Hill near the Vatican, housed numerous people, including 15 Italian-American students trapped after Pearl Harbor, who lived there on the condition that they would not leave until the Liberation and that they would avoid all contact with the seminary students so as not to violate security or expose the seminarians to liability;
- Allied escapers were housed in many cases along with others on the run. For example, the seminary building (Pope's Palace) behind the Pope's own parish church. St. John in Lateran (San Giovanni in Laterano) was filled to the brim with 800 top Resistance leaders, Jews and Allied escapers." (at any one time)

ABBEY OF MONTE CASSINO

The Germans controlled most of the land around this old monastery built high on top of the peak. The German 88mm anti-aircraft guns were pointed down hill. This resulted in devastating the allied troops attacking the mountain. Any attempts by the American forces to use their 90mm anti-aircraft batteries were limited to firing above the horizon. The versatilities of the German 88mms allowed them to be used above and below the horizon.

Most historians are critical of the allies use of heavy air raids that eventually destroyed the monastery because the Germans were not occupying the site at that time. Dr. O'Connor lists the following helpful hints on visiting this battle scene at the present;

"Monte Cassino is in the very southern portion of Rome's province of Lazio just north of the boundary line with Naples' province of Campania. It is about 140 km south of Rome on Via Casilina (Highway 6 and just off of today's A-1 Autostrada toll way). The town of Cassino is on the main rail line to Naples."

"The best way of get to Cassino, the town at the base of the mountain, is an express train from Statione Termini in Rome. If going by train, either leave on the early morning train Sunday and arrive in time for the 10:30 Mass (sung in Gregorian Chant) or go on Saturday and stay overnight in Cassino. Taxis are available at the Cassino train station. The taxi can take you to the Polish cemetery on the hillside across from the Abby and then to the Abbey in time for mass and will return at a prearranged time to bring you back to town and to the British and German cemeteries."

"Check the weather reports and try to go to Monte Cassino on a clear day since it is the view from the abbey and the view of the abbey from the valley (below) that will illustrate the dilemma facing the allies."

"Before catching the train back to Rome you can grab a quick meal in Cassino. Near the train station is some of the best pizza ever. The current town of Cassino is actually centered several hundred meters from the original. The Germans destroyed every structure in Cassino and used the rubble as cover for the devastating ambush of allied troops."

The book, A Loyola Rome Student's Guide to World War II in Rome & Italy, by Dr. O'Connor contains much more about the American Army's experiences during WWII in Italy. He invites anyone interested in his book to email him at philo:conner@earthlink.com to get a pdf of his book.

LOCATING THE CEMETERY OF YOUR FAMILY OR FRIEND

Start with http://www.abmc.gov/cemeteries/cemeteries/sr.php website to contact, American Battle Monuments, with discharge, death or service serial number.

AMERICAN CEMETERIES IN ITALY

SICILY-ROME CEMETERY ANZIO-NETTUNO

7861 heroes WWII

To Get There: The cemetery is open daily 900-1700 except closed Christmas and New Years. It is situated in the coastal town of Nettuno, which is just a few km east of Anzio and 60 km south of Rome via route Via Pointina.

By car: From Rome connect on to the Via Pontina SS148 heading south direction Pomezia then Aprilia and before Latina exit at Velletri-Nettuno. Turn right to Nettuno and follow this road straight some 9 km to the cemetery; park in front of gate on right.

By Railroad: Take the regularly scheduled train from Rome to Nettuno, then a cab Via Santa Maria to cemetery.

THE ANZIO-NETTUNO AMERICAN CEMETERY & LANDING SITES

The cemeteries and landing beaches are about 18 miles south of Rome. Anzio can be reached several ways. One is by taking the metro (train B) to the EUR, Fermi Station and catching an express bus to downtown Anzio. Check with COTRAL, the Lazio provincial bus company, for bus times and routes. There are also trains to Anzio-Nettuno (from Termini Rome R.R. Station). Both the American (Nettuno) and British (Anzio) cemeteries are easily reached by taxi, bus, or foot as are the two local museums commemorating the landing and the liberation. In addition to the 7860 headstones (crosses & star of Davids), marking the resting places of 7861 Americans (two brothers lie side by side in a single grave), there is a set of large marble insets recounting the course of the Italian campaign from Sicily to Rome during which these men and so many other were lost.

The Anzio Museum is located at Via di Villa Adele. Its web link is http://www.anzio.net/davedere/sbarco.htm

The Nettuno museum is at Via della Vittorio II and the telephone number is 06.980.3620.

The 1st, 3rd and 4th U.S. Ranger Battalions took the ports of Anzio and "Yellow" Beach on the southern edge of Anzio in the direction of Nettuno. "Peter" Beach, about 10 km up the coast from Anzio and a couple of kilometers from Nettuno was the "X-'ray" beach landing zone of the American 3rd Infantry Division (the Army unit that most recently was the vanguard of the Iraq War)"

FLORENCE AMERICAN CEMETERY, FLORENCE, ITALY
4402 heroes WWII

To Get There: The Florence, American Cemetery, is located on the west side of Via Cassia, about 7 miles south of Florence. The Rome-Milan A1 autostrada passes near the cemetery. Its Impruneta-Florence exit is two miles to the north.

There is excellent train service to Florence from the principal cities of Italy. It is also served by some of the international trains. The SITA bus station provides frequent bus service along Via Cassia and there is a bus stop conveniently located just outside the cemetery gate. The cemetery is open daily 9 - 5 except Christmas and New Year's Day.

Made in the USA
Middletown, DE
05 January 2019